FACING ATHENS

FACING ATHENS

Encounters with the Modern City

GEORGE SARRINIKOLAOU

NORTH POINT PRESS

A DIVISION OF FARRAR, STRAUS AND GIROUX · NEW YORK

North Point Press
A division of Farrar, Straus and Giroux
19 Union Square West, New York 10003

Illustrations courtesy of Suzy Spence.

Library of Congress Cataloging-in-Publication Data
Sarrinikolaou, George, 1970–
    Facing Athens : encounters with the modern city / by George Sarrinikolaou.
        p.   cm.
    ISBN 0-86547-699-3
    1. Athens (Greece)—Social life and customs.   2. Sarrinikolaou, George,
    1970–   3. Greek Americans—Biography.   I. Title.

DF920.S26 2004
949.5′12076′092—dc22

                                                                    2003019447

EAN: 978-0-86547-699-8

Designed by Debbie Glasserman

www.fsgbooks.com

10   9   8   7   6   5   4   3   2   1

To my mother, Elli, and my sister, Magdalen

CONTENTS

PROLOGUE

I returned to Athens this time to speak of it, and in finding the strength to speak, to reclaim a place for myself in the city where I was born.

Athens was once my world, inhabited by the people who loved me, full of the joys and scars of childhood. But at the age of ten, I emigrated from Athens to New York with my parents and my sister, forfeiting one life for another. My birthplace then became a repository for the past and a reminder of what would never be. No matter that we settled among thousands of other Greeks in Astoria, New York, that I continued to cultivate my Greek and speak it with the intonation of an Athenian, or that I eventually reported on Greek affairs on public radio and in the press. At the moment our New York–bound Olympic Airways jumbo jet took off on that September day, I became a perennial visitor, neither an insider nor an outsider, but one who stares at one's life through glass.

Nearly every year since we left Athens, I inserted myself into the city for a few weeks. At first, I would return in the summer to stay with an aunt and commit small acts of teenage rebellion: riding on the back of an old friend's motorcycle, sampling vodka for the first time at the local discotheque. As time passed, I would come seeking out my estranged father (my parents divorced shortly after we arrived in New York, and my father moved back to Athens), for a friend's wedding, or as a journalist. I would then move about the city looking like many of the other young men my age: tall, lean, olive-skinned, with brown eyes under thick eyebrows. With neither my appearance nor my speech betraying my emigration, I would pretend to be like everyone else being jostled on the bus, perspiring under the sun, breathing in the smog.

My pretense was convincing, but only as long as my contact with others remained superficial. When a friend would introduce me to people sitting around a table as his pal "from America," I wouldn't even get the chance to pretend. Instantly, I would sense the effect of his words. I would become an emigrant again, someone who could not know all that these people assumed I knew a moment before, who did not share what they shared. And this distance assigned to me undermined the validity of anything I had to say about life in Athens. When I once proposed, for example, that Athenians had turned illegal immigrants into scapegoats for the crime in the city, the retort came easily: "What do you know? You don't live here." And if people did not use the American tag to push me away, they saw it as a signal to pull back. In the eyes of the single women who sat around the table, I would be transformed from an eligible bachelor one minute to an impossibility the next. For others, I would become a tourist, and their conversation a stop along my sightseeing tour. So they would just talk around me, leaving me to look on.

I don't know that there is any one reason that Athenians react this way. Perhaps life in the city feels so difficult that it seems impossible for anyone who doesn't experience it every day to understand it. Perhaps it's because people find the "from America" label easier to grasp than my personal history.

Whatever the reason, I never protested others' retreat from me. Instead, rather than engaging the city, I found it easier to remain suspended in my own quiet space made up solely of remembrance and loss. There my memories surfaced over and over again. Countless times I was the boy in Athens who kicked a soccer ball in the square, went to school, saw his newborn sister come home, watched his father's violence and his mother's fright. And numerous times more I wondered about all that I missed for having left, about all that I would never know of my grandparents growing old and the family's children growing up, of friends I never met, and of the man I would have become had we stayed. From this past, both real and imagined, I erected a place to come to each time I was turned away from actual Athens. And I stood there facing the city, my eyes locked on the life that went on without me. The place comforted me, but in it my life was small, restricted.

I have always known that my memories hold more than nostalgia and the nightmares of domestic violence; they store what I love—what I first learned of Athens and its people. And my distance from the city has produced not only a sense of loss, but also a perspective that is different from, but no less clear than, that of anyone who lives there.

It was not until this last journey, however, that I mustered the courage to honor my love of the place and speak of what goes on in the city. Yet I left New York not knowing if I would have enough money to restart my life when I returned, or if I were foolish to think I could write a book.

I arrived in Athens not on a sunny summer day as usual, but on a rainy one in spring. This time, I planned to stay for three months, longer than anytime since I first left. And I lived not with relatives or friends, or at some seaside hotel. Instead I became a lodger, renting a room with a mattress on the floor, a chair, a lamp, and a rusty child's desk. To find the place, I went to Koukaki, a middle-class neighborhood in central Athens, turned right at a garbage dumpster, and walked down an alley that residents there called a street.

From there I would set off each day to walk the city's streets, seeking to imprint a fresh experience alongside the remembered ones. I became one of the pedestrians, the people in Athens who dodge cars. My wanderings began atop familiar ground—the Acropolis—but extended to places few outsiders or even Athenians ever see: a drug dealer's shack on the western edge of town, the prime minister's anteroom. Everywhere, I came across the forces that are shaping Athens today: money, history, immigration, violence. The story I tell focuses on the people who make their lives among all of this. They were the ones who pulled me to the city's center, to the rich northern suburbs, and to the poverty-stricken sections everywhere.

As the traffic whizzed by me, I saw things that I knew lurked there, things that hurt me. I saw my city gripped by greed, corruption, and racism. I saw a few people take for themselves as much as they could, leaving the rest to compete for the little that was left. I spoke with children who sleep on the ground. In the labyrinth that spreads out from the Acropolis, I found young men ready to buy and young women willing to be bought. Here an Iraqi Kurd was dodging the police on his way to Germany, and a Gypsy family was being evicted from a shantytown. I entered crumbling homes, posh suburbs, churches, and my old neighborhoods. Along the way, memories of Athens sprang up all around me, more vivid than ever before. I would distill from them what I could—sometimes love, sometimes pain—anything to keep me going on this journey.

Then another day would end in Athens, the buzzing traffic would grow quiet, the smog would dissipate in the nightly breeze. In the slower pace of evening, I sometimes would grieve for all that I had seen, for something that I had remembered. And then I would walk to my rented room to write, to claim my place in the city, and to add my voice to the next morning's din.

FACING ATHENS

1 THE JOURNEY BEGINS

From the Acropolis, it looks as if a giant—in a moment of boredom, or perhaps disgust—threw his toy houses in the air. Where they landed, modern Athens was formed. Now the toys, in revenge for their neglect, seem to be multiplying, filling every nook of the Athenian basin and slowly climbing the mountains to the north, east, and west. In the crevices between the myriad jagged little white cubes, I look for traces of human life. Instead, my eye spots a blue sign that screams NOKIA. When I focus more intently, I find a stream of cars silently heading north. Only what's left standing of the Parthenon and the Aegean to the south have escaped the giant's sloppy hand. I turn to the ancient temple, honey-colored in the dull sun, and back to the glistening sea to the south, seeking something to counter the architectural frenzy below. Soon enough, I know, I must descend this hill.

It's April, and the tourists scaling the ancient site are few. But even in the off-season, jet travel makes the small crowd polyglot. The mix of tongues is different now than in the latter decades of the twentieth century. The omnipresent German, British, French, and American tourists are now joined by Eastern Europeans. With disposable income, sneakers, and Japanese electronics in hand, Poles, Russians, and other recently Westernized peoples are climbing around the ruins. Ordinary people from disparate lands and I, a displaced native—all of us looking more and more alike—gather here, drawn by a single image. Up close, the Parthenon validates the virtual foundations of life. For a moment, at least, our anxiety dissipates; we have not been fooled. The magic processes that embedded this Athenian logo in our psyches, before we ever stood before it, were benevolent. For some, however, gazing at the actual site must be too much. And so they negotiate the moment through viewfinders, lenses, and digital circuits.

When two Greek men walk by, one explaining to the other the intricacies of his new mobile phone, I think that the Parthenon is becoming more and more necessary for this city. It is not that technological advances have been more disruptive here than elsewhere. If anything, Greeks embraced technologies such as mobile phones and the Internet because they were cool, and because they offered opportunities to circumvent bureaucracy. (It used to take years to get home telephone service in Greece.) Technological change has been accompanied by revolutionary developments in the economy, the physical environment, the social fabric of this city, and even the political geography of the region. Many of these changes have benefited Athens, but they have also created serious problems. People here say that life is rotten. The theme is a favorite of radio disc jockeys and anyone who learns that I am writing about Athens. Nothing works; nothing ever gets done; the government is corrupt; people cheat; traffic is unbearable; crime is on the rise; blame it on the Albanian immigrants.

In such circumstances, it is not so much the Parthenon's beauty, or the strength evident in its survival that is necessary. Rather, it is the sanctity of the place, which beauty and strength only fortify. It is as if the ancient Athenians built this temple with their modern descendants in mind, providing them with a spiritual refuge in their time of need. Athenians send their children on school trips here, they guard the place, charge admission, preserve it, light it up at night, drive around it, damage it with their smog, make love in its shadows, ignore it in their daily perambulations, and take pride in it. Here is the flow of life, "the whole catastrophe" as Nikos Kazantzakis writes in *Zorba the Greek*, everything that these people have. The Parthenon shrinks, becoming part of life, and reigns unperturbed above it all. This duality is the holy spirit of the place, and if you look, you will see the temple radiate.

Early in Kazantzakis's novel, Zorba, in a letter, summons an English friend to Greece to show him a magnificent little green pebble he has found. Had Zorba visited the Parthenon this afternoon, he would have summoned his friend to see the poppies—you'll never see a brighter red—growing alongside the temple's marble pieces that are strewn around the Acropolis. I find one in the Parthenon's shadow, and then a small grove of them under the wooden steps that lead to the exit. Outside the gate, I take the south walkway and head down the hill. Olive and pine trees cover the hillside, but it is the poppies that make the place magical. And, as if the red star-bursts were not enough, chamomile grows here too. Red poppies, white chamomile, green grass, patches of blue-and-white sky, the creamy-golden marble columns showing through the trees: I have walked into a pastoral landscape that stubbornly, serenely claims its space in this concrete city. The swallows, too, know this place. They fly chirping overhead, back from their winter interlude some place warmer, farther south.

> My assignment is to draw a picture of "Spring," but the swallows are really all I can manage. I draw slender, lowercase gammas, whose ends form the birds' scissor-tails. I make them slender for swallows and fatter when I have to draw fish. I try my hand at flowers, a tree, even ants, but I know they are no good. When she decides to help, Mother sits at the kitchen table next to me and draws a bird of a different kind, a sparrow perhaps, perched on my tree. The bird is pretty, and it looks unlike anything I have drawn. That I will have something so pretty as part of my drawing reduces the embarrassment I feel when I think that the teacher will notice I got help with my homework.

A third of the way down the hill, modern Athens begins. At the borderline, a new pedestrian walkway softens the transition between the ancient and the modern. I head west along this path, keeping the Acropolis on my left. The path is deserted—a street musician, up ahead, the only other person on it. In the distance to the east, the clouds drift over Mount Ymittos. For more than twenty years, I have known Athens only during its hot and crowded summers. In April the place has a simpler, introverted feel. A stray dog wanders by. As I approach, the music gets louder. The musician, hunched over a dulcimer, sits by the side of the road. He works the hammers, making an airy music that sounds both familiar and distant. I pull some of the recently circulated euros in coins from my pocket and try to make sense of their value. Before the euro replaced the drachma in 2002, fifty or a hundred of the local currency would have been the right amount to drop in a street musician's hat. The coins in my hand now are in ones and twos. I place the money in this man's knit cap, which lies on the ground before him, and sit a few feet to his right. He goes on playing, never looking up. The music softens my chest; it seems to soften everything. For the first time since my arrival, I let down and breathe deeply.

When he stops playing, we turn to each other and smile. He is in his thirties, with a handsome dark face, black hair, and a neatly trimmed moustache. He wears a worn plaid flannel shirt, blue pants, and no-name sneakers. In Greek, I tell him he plays well. He nods and shakes a cigarette out of a pack of Winstons. When I ask him, he says, in simple Greek, that he's from Persia, and that is where he learned to play the santour. I tell him I live in America. But I don't ask him why he is here, or how he got to Greece from Iran, why he chose to stop in Athens, how he survives, what he hopes to do, or if he misses his home. The answers to these questions would only point to what I already know. Living an immigrant's life is one of the most difficult things a person can do. Being an immigrant in Athens must be especially hard. This city has forgotten that it is itself made up of internal immigrants and Greek refugees. It has forgotten that, for much of the last century, emigrating abroad was the only way to survive for countless Greeks, and that the country's economy relied on the money immigrants sent home. Now Greece, and Athens especially, has unwillingly become an immigrant destination. Greeks call their treatment of the new inhabitants xenophobic, but, really, it's racist.

We sit quietly for a while as he smokes and as I watch some stray dogs try to mount a yellow Labrador retriever, which looks resigned at the end of her owner's leash. The musician picks up one of the hammers with his free hand and begins to play a melody I recognize. It is his way of communicating with me. When he stops, he tells me that the music in Greece and in Persia is the same. But when he puts out his cigarette and begins to play again in earnest, the music speaks of an infinite distance between this spot under the Acropolis and his homeland.

I sleep next to my father on our first night in New York. But I wake up often and peer out the window. The streetlights cast an orange glow on the row of houses across the street and on our faces. Nothing looks familiar; everything seems bigger, uglier. My father and I look at each other, but we don't speak. We are finally in America.

A middle-aged Japanese woman appears just in time to complicate the scene. In full tourist regalia—silly hat, knapsack, camera, and walking shoes—she kneels before the santour and leans her head inches above the undulating hammers. She is so close to the musician that I feel uncomfortable. When, at that close distance, she starts asking him questions in Japanese, her rudeness has me scanning my college learning of multicultural-ism for some adequate definition of tolerance. He nods and keeps playing. When she, with some broken English, manages to have him say that he's from Persia and that he plays the san-tour, I feel like a fool for having asked the same questions. But the bathos of the moment has no end. The word *santour*, to her ears, sounds like Santorini. And she proudly announces that she has visited that Greek island by pointing to herself and re-peating the island's name. The music goes on long enough for the Greek woman with the Labrador to join the show. After a moment, she, too, has a question. In English: "Greek music?" "Persia," he says. "No Persia music," she says. "This Greek mu-sic, Greek." The Japanese woman pulls a few coins out of a change purse and puts them in the hat on the ground. Before leaving, she wants confirmation of her payment, which she elicits by talking to him in Japanese and pointing to the knit cap. He smiles to her as he plays, whereupon she rises, bows, and walks away with her male companion, who has been standing out of view the whole time.

He and I are alone again. The Persian immigrant, who is likely a Kurd, and the Greek immigrant with an American passport are sitting under a pine tree, which grows under the Parthenon, toward which the Japanese tourists head. And then there is the Greek woman. In a city with nearly as many stray dogs as people, she walks a well-fed Labrador down the hill. (The notion that Labradors make the best friends of the urban professional class has apparently traveled beyond the confines of Manhattan.) For a few minutes, all the forces of the world converge: war, survival, economics, technology, art, history, Westernization, development, law. And we, for a moment, give flesh to that unfathomable complexity. But I am here, I tell myself, because of something outside that calculus. Instinctively, I turn to the west, wondering which among those countless houses used to be mine. The sprawl of Athens fades in the haze. The santour player stops and smiles. He tells me he will take some time to tune his instrument. His hands work the strings. I set out again. The road is deserted once more.

Down below, among the jagged little white cubes, a survival experiment is in progress. To repeat the experiment elsewhere, follow these instructions: Crowd half your country's population into one small city; keep unemployment at 10 percent or more; allow unplanned, unzoned development; provide few public services; and encourage corruption. For best results, it is recommended that the people have a long history of economic struggle, political oppression, war (both foreign and civil), occupation, persecution, foreign intervention, and political instability. If your city begins to look anything like Athens, then the experiment is succeeding.

Under such conditions, much of life feels to me like a competition, whose prizes are money, space, sex, even air. In Athens, the winners reward themselves with opulent villas, chauffeured German automobiles, Filipino maids, yachts, casinos, high-priced prostitutes, and, most important, distance from the city center. The closer one gets to downtown, villas turn into apartment buildings, manicured gardens into sooty balconies, big cars into small cars, Filipino maids into Albanian day workers, yachts into ferries, casinos into lottery games, the expensive hookers trafficked from Russia into cheaper ones from Greece and Eastern Europe. And everywhere there are cracks filled with the destitute, the hustlers, the immigrants, the forgotten. No one, though, is ever beyond the game.

Driving in Athens is the consummate event of this contest, with everyone fiercely competing everywhere, operating anything and everything with wheels and an engine. Too many drivers vie for passage through roads that are often too narrow, unlit, unmarked, and playfully wound. Traffic on the major commuting routes can crawl on for hours, making a trip of nine or ten kilometers a maddening experience. In midday at the center, cars move within centimeters of each other, while motorcycles and mopeds dart in between. In the frenzy, pedestrians are only added irritants, obstacles that take up much-needed street surface. Once motorists reach their destination, few find legal parking. And then any available surface, including the sidewalk, is a prime spot.

In spite of the difficulties, Athenians love their cars, so that no matter how hard the government tries to limit driving, it fails. Athens, for instance, seeks to reduce congestion and smog by imposing a driving ban on weekdays. City officials distinguish vehicles based on whether their license plates end in odd or even numbers, and allow downtown access to each category on alternate weekdays. But many car owners respond by buying a second car with alternative plates. Modernized and expanded public transportation has also failed to convince Athenians to give up driving in the city. People have embraced the recently built underground train system—the Metro—but when I ask motorists exasperated by traffic about the possibility of using trains and buses, they consider the notion laughable and tell me that public transportation is slow and unreliable. In their response, I hear the disdain that people reserve for nearly everything associated with the government.

In a country where people must rely on the state for most services, the government has become synonymous with bureaucracy, inefficiency, and corruption. In the city that serves as the seat of that government, then, the automobile represents more than a mode of transportation. It shelters the driver from the perceived or real problems of government as they are manifested in public transportation: the whimsicality of the bus schedule; the rudeness of the driver, a civil servant whose job security is guaranteed; the lack of climate control; the absence of a seat on overcrowded trains and buses. Driving one's own car, one is free, even in gridlock.

> The doors shut and we're off. My uncle drives and my aunt sits next to him. In the backseat, it's tight. Mother and my two cousins, both girls, take up all the space. I will alternate laps and have to duck if we pass a traffic cop. It's illegal to squeeze more than five passengers in this car. I worry about being stopped, but not too much. We're going to the sea.

Confined freedom, comfort under duress, and a false sense of security seem to me the true prizes of this urban game. And if the car does not provide them in ample quantities, then the home certainly does. For a sense of shelter, there are Athenians who would build anywhere. The rest make their homes where they are allowed, and, often, where they will not get caught.

The fickle cityscape tells of a long history where urban planning and zoning have constantly sought to catch up with reality. The location and size of a building often depend on where one owns land and on one's needs. Even now, in peripheral areas such as Penteli and Lagonisi, one popular strategy is to occupy public land or to buy an unzoned plot, build on it, and wait for the government to legalize the structure. The government tends to oblige, especially if an election is approaching, or simply to ignore the illegality. The results are villas nestled in wooded areas, restaurants taking up the city's western waterfront, and shacks clinging to the hillsides. To the inhabitants of these dwellings, the blight on the landscape seems of no concern at all. As long as they can shut their doors to the impinging outside, creating for themselves a safe and quiet spot, they have succeeded. If home building makes for crowded and disorienting conditions, then that's life. But if there is a view, especially of the sea, then that's paradise.

The right house and the right car can yield the game's next prize—the right mate. Cars and houses are status symbols nearly everywhere. But what strikes me in Athens, as opposed to my other home, New York, is how conspicuous the role of money can be in sexual relationships. I tell a male friend that I went on a first date with an Athens native, and he asks me if the woman grilled me about how much money I make. She had, but I had evaded answering. Another woman, a doctor's daughter, tells me that when she marries, she must, at the very least, maintain her station in life. The moneyed young men I meet speak of women with a cynicism that makes them sound like bitter old men. Around a table with the sons of an industrialist, a shoe manufacturer, and a government official, talk is often of girlfriends, wives, and favorite prostitutes. I find little in the conversation that distinguishes each category, except perhaps the extent to which the relationship is openly about money. A prostitute commands a fee, which varies according to the length of her visit and whether she was recently featured on the cover of a magazine (as an aspiring model, or actress, or singer). The transaction with girlfriends and wives is less clear-cut. For these young men, finding a girlfriend or keeping a wife is a function of their bank accounts, cars, country homes, yachts, and earning potential.

Nonetheless, whether for love or money, marriage is still important in Athens, and those around the table who are single expect to marry. Making a family adds another protective layer against the harshness of the city. For my friend Dimitris, marrying his wife, Penelope, translated into home ownership: Her parents considered it their duty to provide the newlywed couple with a place to live. When Dimitris became a father, his parents-in-law helped him buy a house near the beach, so the couple would have a convenient place to go on vacation with the baby. Over a lifetime, a family may also help with child care, finding a job, and negotiating the bureaucracy.

But however tenuous the protection of car, home, and family may be, no one who lives in Athens could ever lack reasons for seeking it. The memories of Nazi occupation, civil war, poverty, and political oppression are still fresh in Athens. And now there is an onslaught of new difficulties. Making a living in a small country with few natural resources has never been easy. But as Greece tries to claim a role in a globalized system of trade and specialized economies, it is not clear what the country's competitive advantage is. Like elsewhere in Europe, much of the shrinking agricultural sector survives because of European Union subsidies. Greece offers an abundance of highly educated young people, many of whom are concentrated in the capital. But the economy, which statistically is improving, has not developed enough to make good use of the population's available skills. Although economic growth in recent years has matched or exceeded that of other European Union nations, inflation has decreased to single digits, and public works projects (a new airport, new highways, modernized railways) have encouraged trade, unemployment still hovers around 10 percent and is far higher for young people. Those who do work are often underemployed.

In the mid-1990s, it seemed as if the stock market would bring economic salvation. Investment returns were often as high as 25 percent. Suddenly, everyone became an investor and every stock held the potential of great fortune. With interest rates plummeting and stock returns soaring, countless Athenians converted their savings into equity. Many went even further, selling property, even borrowing from banks in order to invest. Privately held companies recognized the opportunity to cash in and went public. All over Greece, a new profession—stock brokering—emerged. With few or no credentials, people opened brokerage firms. In Athens, underemployed young men donned suits and imagined they were on Wall Street. In a span of four or five years, speculation drove the Athens Stock Exchange index to double in value. But by 2001, the stock market had essentially crashed. Investors were left feeling duped; many were ruined. One of my uncles, a hardworking immigrant in the United States for some thirty years before retiring to Athens, lost nearly his entire nest egg—$60,000. Greeks blame the government for encouraging them to invest, and for failing to implement adequate stock market controls. Government officials say people ought to have known that investment involved risk.

Political problems compound the economic difficulties. To the east, Turkey represents a constant threat in spite of efforts at rapprochement. As a small country in a dangerous region, Greece seeks protection and support from the North Atlantic Treaty Organization and the European Union, and so often finds itself having to hew to the policies of these organizations at the cost of internal conflict. For example, Greece went along with the European Community decision that sanctioned the breakup of the former Yugoslavia. But the ensuing wars in that country generated such instability and economic damage that the reverberations shook Greece. From the pieces of Yugoslavia emerged Macedonia, a new state that appropriated chunks of Greek history, including Alexander the Great, and which, at least implicitly, claimed Greek territory as its own. Greece countered with a costly trade embargo that obstructed the flow of trade through the Balkans even further. Later, when Kosovo erupted, the war reached within a few kilometers of the Greek border. For many here, the wars were redolent of the Muslim-Christian conflict that raged in the Balkans in the nineteenth and early twentieth centuries. To these people, the notion that the wars to the north pitted the evil Serbs against the defenseless Bosnians rang false; in the treatment of their fellow Orthodox Christian Serbs by the Western allies, Greeks saw reflected their own experiences of powerlessness and injustice.

Mother leads me by the hand through the gates of the Metsovion Polytechnic University in Athens. We walk along the columns that hold up the building overhead. Every so often, we stop in front of a column and read the plastered poster. Each one tells of the student who was shot at that particular spot, the number of bullet wounds, the organs that the bullets struck. Farther inside the courtyard, we see the damaged building, the broken windows. The junta's tanks, I know, crushed the student uprising. But we're here now because the dictators are gone.

As Athenians walk and drive on their streets, they are re-minded daily of the grand forces beyond their control. There are remnants here of the world's major news stories long after they have dropped from the headlines. Pieces of the shattered iron curtain are everywhere—Albanians, Bulgarians, Romani-ans, Poles, and Russians. The men work in construction, often as day workers, or in factories, many off the books. The women clean houses and care for the elderly. Some become strippers or turn tricks. Their children may offer to sell you packs of tissues, or to wash your windshield; others simply beg. Here, too, are the Kurds of Iraq, abandoned by the United States and its allies as Saddam Hussein's forces closed in after the first Gulf War. And, here, of course, are displaced Serbs, who have come in the hope that Greek sympathy will translate into a job. I also find Chinese, Africans, Arabs, Indi-ans, and Pakistanis, all touched somehow by some faraway up-heaval. In a city that was until recently largely homogeneous, the influx of immigrants has been a shock.

For native Greeks, immigrants have become scapegoats, another obstacle in the game. The signs of racism are easy to spot. In searching the newspaper for a place to live, I find ad after ad in which non-Greeks are told not to apply. That so many Athenians invite immigrants into their homes to cook and clean for them, or that so many new homes in the city are now built by non-Greeks, matters little. A taxi driver speaks of criminals and Albanian immigrants as if the two nouns were synonymous. A relative complains that, at the beach, a group of Albanians insisted on speaking among themselves in their native tongue. On television and radio, news broadcasters identify the ethnic origin of crime suspects only if they are not Greek. A storeowner complains that his neighborhood feels like a foreign country. Such racism is even directed against immigrants of Greek descent from Albania and elsewhere in Eastern Europe and the former Soviet Union. Abroad, these Greeks once represented the Greek diaspora, evidence of the far-reaching, civilizing force of Hellenism. Now, repatriated, they, too, are foreigners.

Everywhere the outside pushes in. Under the pressure, I see Athenians taking cover, searching for a means of escape, surviving. The mad, unending, exhausting force of competition flows through the city's streets and carries me with it. Lost, I become an Athenian again, one more in the bobbing crowd. To find my way out, I sift through the old and the new; somewhere here, I tell myself, is what I'm looking for. It's just hard to find.

2 CENTER SPECTER

The Greek word *omonia* (pronounced o-MO-nee-ah) combines the ideas of concord, harmony, and unity. In Greece, whose long history is marked by discord, infighting, and division, the word also suggests the elusiveness of those ideals. And while the spirit of *omonia* has rarely taken hold here, the early planners and architects of modern Athens in the nineteenth century were not discouraged. They weighed the word down with brick and mortar and gave it a central place on the city map, making certain that *omonia* would never escape Athens again. For nearly two hundred years, Omonia Square—now a traffic circle—has physically and symbolically served as the city center. Rather than a downtown, Athens has a center (*kentro*), and Omonia Square lies at the center of the center. But now even this reified form of *omonia* is taking flight.

The signs that the center is losing its hold are not readily apparent. Omonia Square buzzes with traffic. People come from all directions, even from underground as the trains disgorge their loads. The fast-food restaurants on every corner always seem crowded (before Easter, McDonald's is boosting its sales with a menu it's calling *McSarakosti*, literally, "McLent"). All around, the shops, hotels, and office buildings lead visitors to believe that business at the Square remains good. The government has also sought to reaffirm the centrality of Omonia Square in anticipation of the 2004 Olympic Games. The city has built a new Metro hub, has encouraged the renovation of the surrounding neoclassical buildings, and has gotten property owners to take down the tacky signs that used to adorn the building façades. And in the middle of it all, a new pedestrian plaza promises even greater access to the center.

A street map would also reassure one that Omonia Square remains central. With seven wide streets meeting here, this traffic circle determines how much of the city moves. Symbolically, the street names, too, reinforce the sense of *omonia*. Here street naming is completely given up to the concept of nation-building, with every phase of Greek nationhood represented, beginning with the most ancient.

Athenas Street takes its name from Athena, the goddess of wisdom, protector of Athens, and the city's namesake. And if the name were not enough to remind the passerby of Greece's mythology and ancient history, then the unobstructed view of the Acropolis from this street does. Traces of the ancient past also survive in Stadiou Street, named after the ancient Panathi-naikon Stadium of Herod Atticus. The street name and its ref-erent recall the Greek ideal of "sound body, sound mind," and the value placed on athletic competition for the sake of glory alone.

The pagan gives way to the Christian at Agiou Konstanti-nou Street, named after Constantine the Great. The sanctified Roman Emperor signals the beginning of a historical span (A.D. 324–1453) to which contemporary Greeks often look as they ponder their religion, their ties to the East, and their history of struggle against the Ottoman Empire and modern-day Turkey, a bitter rival despite entreaties from both sides. Over this pe-riod, the Roman Empire was recast as the Byzantine, becom-ing decidedly Greek and Christian. Constantine triggered the change when he issued the Edict of Milan in A.D. 313, ending the persecution of Christians in the Roman Empire, which in-cluded Greece. Some ten years later, he transferred the seat of the empire eastward to the city that took his name, Constan-tinople, or modern-day Istanbul. And then he himself con-verted to Christianity on his deathbed. With Christ on their side, the Greek-speaking peoples of the ensuing Byzantine Empire achieved a level of geographic and cultural domination that they had been unable to attain since the reign of Alexan-der the Great (340–323 B.C.). With ferocious enemies coming from the papal West and the Islamic East, Greek history of that thousand years is also one of survival, a series of battles that would decide not only territorial control but also the ex-tent to which Greek language and tradition, and the Greek Orthodox faith, would continue.

The reemergence of a self-ruled Greek entity after the fall

of Byzantium to the Ottomans in 1453 is memorialized by 3 Septembriou Street, which marks the revolt of September 3, 1843, against the autocratic rule of King Otto and the subsequent signing of the first Greek constitution. The avenue named after the Greek statesman Eleftherios Venizelos extends official history to the 1920s. It was then that Venizelos successfully negotiated the northward expansion of Greece, and extended Greek sovereignty to Turkish- and Bulgarian-controlled areas inhabited by Greek-speaking peoples. But Venizelos's name is also redolent of a period in the country's history known as the Megalos Dihasmos, or the Great Division. With Venizelos as their leader, the so-called Republicans were pitted against the Royalists. In a move to instill *omonia* over this divisive past, Athens recently renamed another of the streets leading to the Square after Venizelos's political nemesis, Panagis Tsaldaris. In dubbing the street Tsaldaris, the authorities not only gave voice to the political sentiment that favored the Royalists, but also championed a politician known to compromise for the good of the nation. The streets named after Venizelos and Tsaldaris were previously named after the university (Panepistimiou) and the port of Piraeus (Piraios), respectively, and Athenians habitually use these former names, maintaining the symbolic ties to two other important foundations of Greek nationhood: letters and maritime commerce.

National concord and harmony are preserved as this short course in Greek history ends with an event about whose glory there is no disagreement—commemorated by 28 Octobriou (October) Street—the day in 1940 when Greece rejected Mussolini's ultimatum to surrender. In so doing, the country entered the Second World War on the Allied side, defeating the invading Italians before capitulating to the Germans. With the ensuing Nazi occupation, however, there began a long period of discord from which it is difficult to pluck a noncontroversial street name. The period includes the fractious Greek resistance against the Germans, collaboration with the Nazis, a civil war between communist-led rebels and U.S.-backed government forces, the persecution and execution of leftists, the emergence of a brutal dictatorship that further widened the gap between the left and the right, and periods of acrimony between the two leading political parties—the conservative New Democracy and the Panhellenic Socialist Movement (PASOK). On the map, the straight lines that lead to the neat little circle cannot account for such history.

But as I step onto the Square in the middle of the afternoon, I sense decentralizing forces stronger than the intentions of urban planners and official historians. Around me, I know, Athens is sprawling in all directions, making any notion of a center ludicrous. Within the circle, I feel I am being pulled in all directions. The people's faces point me to the Balkans, Eastern Europe, Africa, the Middle East, Central and Southeast Asia, and to places I cannot even guess. Here are two men in their thirties—perhaps from Bangladesh, perhaps brothers—who seem to be carrying all their belongings in three canvas bags. I catch them in a photograph, standing in the midst of a moving crowd, looking worried and lost. The immigrants have made Omonia Square the place where they work, hustle, meet, and wonder what the next day will bring. The old Greek street vendors, whom I always remember being here, keep them company. These wizened men somehow survive by shining shoes, selling lottery tickets, and *koulouria*—the Greek version of the pretzel. Among the immigrants and the old men move Gypsies, drug pushers, and Greeks heading elsewhere. But the spirit of *omonia*, which is to imbue the city with the enduring Greekness that informs the surrounding street names, seems long gone. Waves of immigrants, crime, drug use, and poverty make the center a point in flux. If there is a unifying and harmonizing force here, it is the shared struggle to survive.

The symbolic power built into Omonia Square stems from a national fantasy made up of ancient glory, Christianity, liberation, and national achievement. Each episode of the fantasy carries a lesson in the importance of *omonia*; and the parts together are supposed to generate this elusive power. But now on the Square, the fantasy is difficult to believe. The newcomers have brought their own histories and religions. Although they are still powerless to alter the official story, their presence alone is shaking Athens.

From the Square, the forces of change push outwards; the essence of Greekness is shifting not only in Athens, but throughout Greece. Still, the Athenians I talk to—friends, strangers, and relatives—seem to think that they can outdistance the changes. Some have not been to Omonia Square in years, or they won't go back, deterred by the underclass, the heroin addicts, the hustlers. When I announce my plans for a nocturnal visit to Omonia Square, friends advise me to reconsider. People speak of the Square as an area they have conceded to an invading army. Busy as they are trying to make a living and raise their children, I don't blame them for turning away, but their retreat from the center makes life feel tight and circumscribed.

The government helped create an image of the center under siege by transforming the Square into a detention and deportation point for undocumented Albanian immigrants. For years in the 1990s, the police would daily round up the Albanians, put them on buses, and drive them to the border, hundreds of kilometers away. The strategy was futile. A porous border and resourceful smugglers meant that those deported would shortly find their way back to Athens. The 1997 collapse of a nationwide investment pyramid scheme in Albania marked a turning point in Greek immigration policy. Living conditions in Albania, among the poorest countries in the world, worsened as people lost their savings. Lawlessness ensued as mobs broke into military caches and absconded with the stockpiles of arms. News reports said that some half a million military weapons were in the hands of civilians. The violence posed a threat to Greece, which recognized that a way to counter Albania's turmoil would be to let Albanian immigrants work and send their earnings back home. By this point, the Greek government had also come to recognize that its deportation strategy was not only costly, but ineffective. Besides, ordinary Greeks found in Albanian immigrants cheap labor, which they could put to use in building and cleaning their homes, and in working their fields. The result has been a surreal turnaround. The Greek government, using radio and television commercials, has been inviting undocumented immigrants to apply for so-called green cards (the color redolent of the Greek immigrant experience in the United States), which afford them legal residence and the right to work for a year. Immigrants can renew the card each year if they can navigate the tortuous bureaucratic process and afford the fee of about $125.

> The cure for my flat feet is to be found at the Bakakos Pharmacy in Omonia Square. It's the time of the year when I have outgrown my shoe inserts and need to get new ones. The pharmacist makes me stand barefoot on a blank piece of paper and draws the outline of my foot with a pen. Inserts make wearing soccer sneakers impossible. I dread another year of having to play in regular shoes.

The authorities have now turned from the deportation of immigrants to the sweeping away of undesirables as part of the Square's beautification. Immigrants, junkies, and prostitutes who have run-ins with the police here end up in nearby neighborhoods such as Metaxourgio, an inner-city slum far enough away to be out of tourists' view and poor enough so that complaints about the newcomers won't register with the government. And while in Omonia Square the government is fashioning the image of a revitalized Athens, it is in Metaxourgio that the new city is in full view. Everywhere there are the crumbling, sooty, neoclassical homes of an urban middle and working class who fled to the suburbs decades ago. The buildings are now either boarded up or rented to those who could not get away, as well as to the countless new arrivals. On the ground floors, there are car-repair shops, wholesalers of Chinese-made junk, and Arabic cafés. I see a man smoking a water pipe in one of them as I walk by.

On a side street converted to a walkway, I find three Greek men sitting on a stoop. Two of them seem to be in their early fifties; the third is older, perhaps a retiree, who holds a white handkerchief over a tracheotomy. We begin to talk and they tell me about their neighborhood. So many buildings are abandoned, they say, because residents left when Metaxourgio filled up with foreigners. That assertion, I know, is false. Greeks themselves turned this neighborhood into a slum much earlier. It was the move to the suburbs, precipitated at least in part by the onslaught of internal immigrants who crowded central Athens—people such as these men most likely—that transformed the neighborhood. The foreign immigrants moved in simply because they could. Instead of arguing this point, though, I just listen. The men tell me that many Albanians and Gypsies used to reside in the area, but that now Pakistanis are replacing them. This history is recounted as one of deterioration and bitterness. When I try to delve deeper into the causes of their anger, to ask what it is that the immigrants do to them, I am met with hostility. "Why," one man snaps, "are you on the side of the foreigners?" "I'm only trying to understand," I say. And now they offer a complaint I have heard elsewhere: that they cannot sleep with their windows open as they used to. The implication is that immigrants burglarize homes by entering through the windows. "When we complain," one man says, "they call us racists. But if people saw what we see, they would be as angry as we are." In a raspy voice, the man with the tracheotomy says that their Muslim neighbors start their wedding feasts on Sunday and party until Thursday. Not that he has a problem with them, he assures me. It's just that it used to be that everyone was of the same ethnicity and religion in the neighborhood, and they all got along. With the foreigners here, that idyllic past is no more. They reveal to me that the locals have formed something of a vigilante force to chase away the unwanted. From this spot here, they say, it is forbidden for Albanians to pass.

None of these three men looks especially intimidating, but all represent that part of the electorate to which the far-right is appealing for support throughout Europe. In Athens, one fringe neofascist party is trying to capitalize on the anti-immigrant sentiment by promising voters a "Clean Greece." I decide not to ask my interlocutors about their political affiliations, and instead watch a couple of junkies walk by. The man with the tracheotomy says that they all feel sorry for the junkies and leave them alone. When I ask about the area's drug trade, they say that it's vigorous, but that it causes few problems because Metaxourgio serves simply as a meeting place for buyers and sellers. Omonia Square used to be the meeting place, but now it has moved here.

I leave them to keep warm in the afternoon sun, on the lookout for Albanians, and head back to Omonia. Of the seven roads leading away from the Square, I choose Athenas Street, thinking that a new way to make sense of the center may lie with the ancient goddess. I am drawing near the Acropolis when a woman in her forties offers to sell me a pack of cigarettes. Her clothes are dark and dowdy, out of fashion. Like many Greek women, she has dyed her dark hair a lighter color, but hers is a dull reddish-blond, missing the trendy blond highlights. I don't smoke, but I pay one euro and gain ownership of some Karelia Lights. When I ask, she tells me that she's from Russia. And when I press her to be more specific, she tells me that she's from Georgia. "Do you know it?" she asks. "I do," I say and again ask her where. "From Tiflis," she says. "Do you know it?" "I do," I say, and she begins to walk away. "We *were* from Tiflis," she corrects herself. "But now . . . " She lets that fragment hang in the air behind her as she looks around for the next customer. Now she's from a country that she always considered her own, until she got here. For centuries, Greeks have lived around the Black Sea, maintaining their ethnic identity and serving to native Greeks as reminders of the glorious days of ancient Greece and the Byzantine Empire. When the Soviet Union collapsed and with it the Soviet economy, Greece offered to repatriate its distant brethren. But while repatriation has spared the Greeks of the Black Sea many of the legal barriers facing other immigrants, they are marginalized nonetheless. In Athens, people call them Russo-Pontians, signaling their connection to Russia and to Pontus (the Black Sea). For my interlocutor and the other women like her standing nearby, repatriation has meant selling smuggled cigarettes out of handbags.

With the pack in my hand, I walk by a group of some twenty men who look as if they are from the Middle East. They are sitting on a short wall that separates the sidewalk from the small park next to City Hall. I make eye contact with one who is not engaged in the group's conversation. Like the others, he hasn't shaved for days and looks gaunt and tired. "Friend," I say in Greek, "do you smoke?" "How much?" he asks, stone-faced. By now, I have the group's attention. "I don't want them," I say, extending the pack to him. He takes the cigarettes, drops them in his jacket's inside pocket, and smiles as if he just got away with something. To the group, I am clearly a fool, giving cigarettes away for free.

After City Hall, Athenas Street is lined with shops selling cheese, cured meats, fruits, and vegetables. Here are the entrances to the city's fish and meat markets—dark, cavernous spaces from which the voices of the vendors, and the odors of fish and meat spill out into the street. The place feels familiar, and I just drift with the crowd. But a light tap on my arm makes me stop and turn.

A man I recognize as belonging to the group a couple of blocks back is gesturing to me for a cigarette. I shrug to show him that I have no more. Still, he walks beside me as if he wants to tell me something. Unlike his comrade to whom I gave the cigarettes, he has a kind face. And now, looking at him, I regret that I hadn't seen him first. He is especially thin. At about six feet, he is my height, but he looks about forty pounds thinner. His clothes appear clean, cheap, and well worn. A belt with a shiny gold buckle holds his pants up. To get him started, I ask him, in Greek, where he is from. The answer is "Kurdistan," a place that's difficult to find on any contemporary map. "What part of Kurdistan?" I ask. "Iran, Iraq, or Turkey?" "Iraq," he says. We fall silent, but keep walking. Now I try asking him how long he has been in Greece and where he lives in the city. But he doesn't understand me. I switch to English; it doesn't do any good. He responds to my attempts with a word I don't understand at first. But when he repeats it once or twice, I realize that he is saying "Allemagne." He is headed to Germany. Shortly, I learn that he does know one English word. "Police," he says, pointing to a cop a few feet away and making a gesture suggesting trouble. With a nod I try to tell him not to worry. But a couple of steps later he stops and wants to turn back. We shake hands and I wish him good luck. He doesn't understand, so I make a fist in front of my stomach to try to signal fortitude. I don't think he understands the gesture, but he makes the same gesture back to me. Then he's gone.

The next day, I return to where I had first seen the Iraqi Kurds, but I don't find this man among them. A Greek newspaper vendor nearby tells me that the Kurds wait around to be picked up for odd jobs. "They take them," the vendor tells me reassuringly. I wait around and eventually see a Greek man huddling with a young Kurd to close the deal for a day's work. Of all the people to be exploited, Kurds enjoy something of a special status here. That Turkey, the archrival of Greece, persecutes its Kurdish population makes Greeks more sympathetic toward these immigrants. Never mind that factions of Turkish, Iranian, and Iraqi Kurds have often clashed. In Athens, to be a Kurd is to share something of the Greek experience in dealing with Turkish brutality.

Up the street from the Kurds, immigrants whose suffering is unrelated to Turkey try a different way to make a living. On Sofocleous Street, a narrow pathway perpendicular to Athenas Street, Gypsies, Chinese, Pakistanis, Eastern Europeans, and Russians are giving commerce a go. On one side of the street, they have set up the semblance of a flea market, selling Chinese-made trinkets, dirty old clothes, and face tissues. A few have small tables, but most spread out their merchandise on the sidewalk. Some of the vendors have their families with them. I see women nursing children, preparing meals, often just sitting on the ground. Other sellers—sullen, black-clad old men and women—seem never to have had families at all. At midday, the road is filled with Greeks—prospective customers—but most of them seem to have come here to patronize the Greek fruit and vegetable vendors on the opposite side of the street.

> Taking the hand of my aunt Vasso, I know this will be another whirlwind jaunt through Athenas Street and the surrounding market. When we leave her hotel, the rush begins. As long as I keep up and hold on, I know I will be rewarded. We whiz by cheese stores and windows filled with sausages. Once in a while, we stop in stores with heaping sacks of rice, lentils, candies, and nuts. If no one is looking, I immerse my hand in the rice and feel its coolness. But soon we are off again, crossing narrow streets filled with the smells of oregano, sage, and chamomile. My aunt is now holding plastic bags in one hand and my hand in the other. Our spree ends at the toy store—a dark, narrow place with board games toward the back. This time I walk away with "Monopoly" tucked under my arm.

I return to Omonia Square near midnight. This time, I decide to take the Metro, to approach the center underground. Deep within its core, I tell myself, there may be something I missed on the surface, some essence that can keep this city centered. But the designers of the station must have been expecting me. They mock my quest with an art installation called *Oura*, a word that in Greek can mean either a line of people or a tail. A long canvas, treated with photographic chemicals, shows a series of human shadows. The installation is part of a larger work called *Phantasmagorias of Identity*. I have come looking for an optical illusion in a shifting place, where the people might as well be shadows.

Up above, those who have survived the day try their luck at night. A junkie shuffles through the few remaining passersby asking for a smoke. Of the vendors, only the Pakistanis are still at work. They have mobile phone covers for sale if you need them. Weathered men are shutting down the newspaper stalls, while a film crew is setting up. A transvestite walks purposefully to the corner, but then saunters back. Outside a fast-food restaurant, two cops question a group of immigrants and then move on. Across the street, some junkies are holding on until their next fix. Men and women huddle together, whispering, making deals. In their midst, a street cleaner, in a bright orange vest that reads "Municipality of Athenians," is spraying the sidewalk with a high-pressure hose. He points the jet of water heedlessly, as if there were no one around him. The junkies move out of the way, and I move with them. Another passerby, a man probably headed home, doesn't get out of the way in time and gets his shoes sprayed. He threatens to turn the hose on the street cleaner, who ignores the threat and keeps on spraying. City Hall is paying him to keep the city's center looking clean, and he'll be damned if he will fail to do the job. Again, I turn the corner at Athenas Street. A young Greek woman, stoned, propositions me. We both walk on.

I head home through the dark and deserted streets of the market. Behind me the government is battling misery with police, public works, and high-pressure hoses. If the government is prevailing, then scrubbed sidewalks and illuminated building façades are the only signs of its success. Over the junkies, the immigrants, and the poor, the national fantasy still looms. The city's vibrant past is evidenced in the restored neoclassical buildings, and the nation's future promise in the modern Metro station. I wonder if any of the people who drive by are fooled. But then I think that most Athenians may never even see the place for years. For them, attempts at nostalgia and cleanliness probably come too late. They have written off the Square as dangerous, polluted, and foreign. If they are holding on to some Greek essence, then they have found its source elsewhere.

But in Athens, I find no place truly different from Omonia Square. There are, it seems to me, only varying degrees of unease and ways of coping. A friend moved farther away; a cousin is pondering private school for her daughters; my aunt and uncle installed an alarm system; their neighbors bought German shepherds to use as guard dogs; a group of pensioners I meet on the street tells me that they have put bars on their windows. The city's social transformation is something from which to take cover; the home is the last piece of the city over which one has some control. But the effect is isolating, and very much unlike the spirit of *omonia*.

3 · GOOD LIFE

From Athens, the road to paradise is lined with stout glass towers, housing banks, multinational corporations, and expensive appliance stores. This is Kifisias Avenue, the city's pathway to the northern suburbs, or better, the Athenian heaven on earth. Here, only the good are allowed entry. And there is never any doubt about who the good are. They are the rich, the recently moneyed, and their admirers—the upwardly mobile professional class. While all who live here are good, of course, some are better than others. The better one is, the farther north one gets to live. Virtue is rewarded with distance from the problems of the city center. But as if to disguise this simple formula, as if to appease those who aspire to a better and more northerly place, but who are, alas, unworthy, Paradise, or Paradisos, is among the first suburban havens one encounters as one heads away from the center. Friends who live here assure me that the name predates the development of the area into a desirable suburb, that the moniker is no marketing ploy. I try to get them interested in the irony, but fail.

At first glance, there is little here to justify the neighborhood's lofty name. No angels singing overhead, no elaborate gate, not even a sign ushers me into Paradisos. Only the horseback-riding club that I see as I veer right off Kifisias Avenue suggests that I have crossed some invisible threshold. I am now in a section of the city where there is enough room, money, and time to re-create the rural or premodern experience of riding horses. I, myself, enter on foot, but soon realize that Paradisos, like the rest of Athens, is really meant for those who drive. The sidewalk ends after the club, and I am now the only pedestrian, walking opposite traffic on a road with several blind curves. Parked cars to my left often push me farther into the road than I care to go, even if this is paradise. And just as in the city to the south, here, too, apartment buildings have sprouted where lower one- and two-story buildings had once stood. But people here seem to have learned from at least one mistake of their southern neighbors. The apartment buildings are set back from the street, and they are surrounded by small gardens. Having for weeks now lived on a street so narrow that sunlight reaches my window only when the sun is directly overhead, this innovation does seem to me a bit heavenly.

I walk the awkward streets of Paradisos thinking of my

friends who are raising their young son here. The couple grew up in Pangrati, a densely built, crowded neighborhood of the urban middle class in central Athens. But when their turn came to make a family of their own, the move to the suburbs and away from the city was automatic. Paradisos afforded them amenities largely unavailable in the center: a garage in their apartment building, a wide balcony with a view extending beyond the building next door, and distance from the noise, the crime, the immigrants, and the sooty air. All of these together produce the allure that comes from living in the north. By simply relocating a few miles north of their childhood homes, my friends were already doing better than their parents.

The scene on the streets in the late afternoon, however, makes me doubt the extent of the improvement. Haphazard new building construction has created enough problematic intersections and narrow, winding roads that traffic is now snarled in the middle of suburbia. Drivers, in various states of exasperation, sit in a long, slow-moving line of cars. The problem, I find out, is up ahead where this line of cars must enter a two-way road perpendicular to them. At the intersection, there is neither a traffic light nor a stop sign. And so Paradisos drivers resort to a game of chicken, darting in each other's way and betting the other car will stop. Winners of this game get to enjoy another day of suburban comfort.

It is only when I make my way farther north, to the aristocratic section of Kifisia, that I gain a true appreciation of this sort of suburban life. Kifisia is the home of old money, the historic haven for Athenian aristocracy. Here the streets are lined with stately villas rising behind stone walls and smart-looking apartment buildings with neatly pruned gardens. Even the trees look as if they sense that this is no ordinary ground they grow on, rising taller and blooming fuller than anywhere else I've seen in Athens. There are lush eucalyptus trees, tall cypress trees, and swaying palm trees that add a touch of the exotic. And everything—from the trees to the elegant architecture—seems old, making it easy to believe that the place has and always will be rich. Yet an insidious force acting on Kifisia is both feeding on and undoing the area's exclusivity. That force is the expanding upper class—a crop of new money that is buying its way through the barriers of exclusion and distance. Kifisia's expensive shops and restaurants provide the forum for this transition; it is in the Pizza Hut, housed in an old mansion, and at the French and Italian boutiques down the street where the new money is closing in on the old. And it's where the distance between city center and suburb is shrinking.

I, myself, am sitting in the fanciest Häagen-Dazs café there is, where the waiter keeps my water glass filled and asks me if everything—the glass dish of vanilla ice cream and the espresso—is to my liking, and where the bill comes in a supple leather holder. On a weekday afternoon, the café is nearly empty. Only occasionally do expensive-looking couples come in for a break from one of Kifisia's numerous mini shopping malls. These new store clusters, with names such as "Splendor" (*Egli*) and "Palms" (*Finikes*), are invariably built around sweet little courtyards, with neat hedges, nascent palm trees, benches, fountains, marble walkways, and antique-looking lampposts. Here is all of Kifisia—the tradition, the affluence, and the privilege—broken down and reassembled in the vernacular of commerce. The courtyard is meant to offer a seamless transition from the abundant gardens around the villas to the mall, and the high prices to reinforce the distance between Kifisia's dwellers and the rest of the city. Shopping becomes a conduit for experiencing one's riches; it validates wealth. But the mall effect comes off so forced, so artificial that it hints of an anxiety that no item from the Christian Dior boutique can assuage. At the mall, the new money—merchants, dealers, and importers—sells to the old money, which buys to bolster its sense of wealth, while enriching those who, in their sheer numbers and lack of nobility, pose a threat to aristocratic status. (The MaxMara women's clothing boutique captures the paradox well. Resembling a miniature Moorish castle, the store's architecture seems so self-conscious of its fantastical nature that the effect is more kitsch than glamorous.) In turn, the nouveaux riches find at the mall their own validation. They, too, can now shop with the best of them. And so commerce becomes the great equalizer, as a place like Kifisia's Bulgari reduces all distinction between old and new into a simple question of money. One belongs in Kifisia if one has the money to shop.

On the way back from the beach, my uncle takes a detour from the congested national highway. Now, in his Soviet-made red Lada, we are rolling down the widest streets I have ever seen in any neighborhood. I know this is no ordinary place because the roads are tree-lined and the houses have walls around the properties. This is Kifisia, someone says, and I feel as if we are someplace where we do not belong. At an intersection, everyone admires a car that crosses in front of us. It's a Jaguar, they say.

In the afternoon heat, four stray dogs sleep curled up on the cool marble doorstep of the Oxette boutique. And I begin to think that, caught in this parasitic relationship, perhaps Kifisia's rich fail to see that commerce is also inviting the outside in. Down the street from the local McDonald's and behind the Bulgari, a family of Gypsies sits on the sidewalk begging. Away from the stores, I see American-style graffiti scrawled on walls. *Sin* reads one such marking across the Villa Elli's heavy iron gate; the other writings are legible only to their authors. Farther on, in the Kefalari section of Kifisia, anyone with a handful of euros can share the experience of the local residents sitting down to dinner in their villas by simply entering the area's Pizza Hut. The restaurant's sign hangs on the most unhutlike of buildings: an elegant four-story structure, where fortunate diners can enjoy their junk food on the veranda. The takeover of aristocracy by the behemoth of commerce seems complete to me here. Not only has a fast-food chain priced the aristocrats out of this building, but Pizza Hut, in its omnipresence, is making the experience of dinner in Kifisia the same as nearly everywhere else in Athens. So even if one cannot make it all the way here, one can order the stuff to eat at home and feel gratified knowing that one is living life as in the suburban north.

For those whose money cannot buy the separation from the city that Kifisia once offered, or those for whom there is no room here, suburbs farther north have been accommodating. One such place is appropriately named Politia, or State, since it is something of a distinct entity within the city limits—a community whose residents' vast wealth sets it apart as only money in the hands of the nouveaux riches can. Whereas money in Kifisia afforded its residents the means to create a sense of elegance about the place, in Politia, everything seems to be about money itself. The villas here are larger, their gates are higher, and the presence of servants more visible. The effect is that of garish extravagance, as if everything in Politia were there to reflect opulence rather than to serve a useful purpose.

Politia is built on a hillside whose last trees are being cleared to make way for new construction. To get there, I take a small, nearly empty bus from Kifisia. From my back-row seat, everything outside seems quiet. When a gate to one of the mansions opens, I see a Filipino maid mouth a few words to her employer. It's the middle of Saturday afternoon, and the streets are deserted, except for some late-model sports cars driven by young men in polo shirts and sunglasses. It is only when the bus reaches the highest point on its route and swings around that the scene changes. Dozens of young people are taking their coffee at the Best Friends café. The Politia Tennis Club, a widely recognized Athenian symbol of exclusivity, is across the street. At this point, the bus again swings to the left, and makes its final stop before heading back down the hill. I decide to stay on as the bus fills up. I am guessing that the driver and I are the only native Greeks on board. And now I understand why a bus would be allowed to drive through this neighborhood in the first place. It's a little after three o'clock. Quitting time for the area's immigrant workers must have come just minutes before.

Now to my right and left sit middle-aged Albanian men. From the dirt caked in the cracks of their fingers and under their fingernails, I can tell they work as gardeners or as builders. The air is thick with the smell of bodies that have been hard at work. Few speak. Those who can keep their eyes open, stare blankly out the window at the grand homes we pass. Albania, by all accounts one of the most miserable places on earth, is a few hours' drive to the northwest. For a moment, the distance between there and here seems interminable. But soon I realize that the misery is here; it has arrived in the hard faces of these workers, in their colorless and mismatched clothes. The misery is bused in and out of Politia; it enters the gardens and drips its sweat in the brick and mortar that builds and maintains these villas. The proximity of rich and poor seems to crack Politia's polished façade; something about the manicured hand of the villa's mistress dipping into a Chanel purse to pay her Albanian gardener undermines her elevated image in my mind. Here is a weakness, I think, a need revealed. Politia is not rich enough to shield itself from the misery. This Garden of Eden needs the cheap labor to keep it watered and pruned.

Politia is only one more variation in an endless history of dependency between the rich and the poor. And what happens here is neither as brutal nor as overtly exploitative as other chapters of that history—say, the relationship between plantation owners in the American South and their African slaves, or between northern hemisphere industrialists and their cheap labor in the South. Here are simply some wealthy suburbanites paying some poor immigrants a fraction of what they would have to pay native Greeks to do the same jobs. Still, the scene gnaws at me as if I have been confronted with this sort of indecency for the first time. Perhaps it's because I know that some of the residents of Politia are themselves just a generation removed from the sort of poverty that hounds their immigrant servants; perhaps because of this country's long history of misery and immigration. From this close proximity, the good life in Politia, in all of the northern suburbs, seems shameful. Perhaps because this is my city.

4 OUTSIDE PARADISE

On the road that runs along the west side of the Olympic Stadium, two boys play a game that reminds me of stray dogs running after cars. The boys stand on the sidewalk, which also serves as a parking lot for the nearby train station, and jeer at passing vehicles. When there is a break in traffic, one of the boys darts into the road on his little bicycle, makes a wide loop, and returns to the starting spot. The other boy runs behind his friend. Their names are Panayiotis and Jafir. Neither looks to be older than six.

I stand behind them and kneel down to take their picture. In the frame, the boys stand in the foreground and off center. Their faces and hands are dirty; their clothes look like hand-me-downs. Weeds grow at Panayiotis's feet, which are clad in sandals that appear too small. The sidewalk and the road stretch desolate and dusty for some one hundred meters. On either side of the photograph run fields of weeds that meet at a cluster of trees in the distance. A truck is coming around the bend. I photograph the boys once while they are still focused on the traffic flow. But soon they turn and give me shy, inquisitive stares. Showing them the camera is good enough for Panayiotis, who steps forward and offers me a big smile. Jafir, who looks younger and rides the bicycle, still seems puzzled. To put them at ease, I start asking them the silly questions adults ask of kids. Are they good children? Yes, they are. Do they go to school? Panayiotis does, someplace up the road. Jafir now speaks up, but he uses a language I don't understand.

I have come here to learn about the Gypsy encampment on the field that extends beyond this sidewalk. I have seen the shanties from the road and have seen men and women walking about. But I have not had the nerve to enter the camp. Instead, I have lingered on the sidewalk, and I had nearly walked away before spotting the boys. That there are no houses around, that the boys wear worn and dirty clothes, and perhaps even that they play so recklessly make it easy to see that they live in the nearby field, that they are Gypsies. And that they now stand on this sidewalk, outside of the camp, which feels so insulated and closed off to me, saves me from my own cowardice. By speaking with these children, I think, I will have touched that other world, if only for a moment.

I grew up afraid of Gypsies, feeling an aversion to them that abounds in Greek culture. To be a Gypsy here is to be untouchable. (Near the Kifisia train station, I stand on line to buy a cheese pie, the local fast food. A Gypsy mother, who has the same idea, is ahead of me. The man serving her does not bother to hide his disgust for her, and he is careful not to touch her hand in the transaction. The mother seems not to notice.) Calling someone a *Gypsy* in the Greek vernacular is to conjure up the cultural image of a life characterized by filth, poverty, vagrancy, and a complacency with such a lifestyle, which other Greeks disdain. People tolerate limited interactions with Gypsies—employing them to work their fields, buying the fruit and vegetables they sell off the back of pickup trucks, even giving a few coins to those who beg on the streets. The rest of the time, the combination of racism and insular Gypsy culture relegate this group to the city's margins. One large Gypsy community lives near a garbage dump in Ano Liossia, on the city's western periphery; I also find Gypsies in the center, living in crumbling homes that Greek families left behind when they moved to the suburbs.

> From the back yard and through the fence, I see a group
> of six or seven women descend the hill at the end of
> the road. I know they are Gypsies from their colorful
> clothing, their long black hair, and their brown skins.
> Once they reach the houses, they split up and begin to
> ring doorbells. To those who answer, the women offer to
> tell their fortunes. I feel the urge to run and hide.

My small talk with Panayiotis and Jafir ends when a blue sedan pulls up. The driver is a young Gypsy man who looks at the children and then at me through the passenger-side window. I answer his look by telling him that I have just been chatting with the boys. He nods, says something to Jafir, and pulls the car onto the sidewalk and down a driveway hidden behind a few trees. Having parked the car, he emerges looking less suspicious. And when I tell him that I'd like to interview him for a piece I am writing about Athens, he becomes friendly. Keeping a vigilant eye on the boys and their traffic game, he tells me that his name is Mouchi (pronounced MOO-chee), that he is twenty-five years old, and that he has three children—a girl and a boy as well as Jafir. To my Americanized sensibility, he seems too young to have three children. But I also know that Gypsies tend to marry young—the girls as early as eleven—and that they have big families. It is this next item of information Mouchi offers me, however, for which I am not prepared. His family and the rest of the people living in the field are not only Gypsies; they are also from Albania. In Greece, I could not imagine a worse fate, a double dose of discrimination and social exclusion. Where to be a Gypsy is to be filthy, to be Albanian is to be criminal. Getting through Greek society, shouldered with both of these ethnic modifiers, seems to me an impossible task.

Still, Mouchi says he is safer in Greece than he was in Albania. The good thing about Albania, he says, is that Gypsies were free to build their shacks anywhere. But then people got guns. "You talk to them and they just shoot you," he says, making a pistol gesture with his hand. Violence spread throughout Albania in 1997, when angry mobs raided military arsenals following the collapse of an investment pyramid scheme. Some five hundred thousand weapons were said to have been stolen and to be circulating among the country's three and a half million people. The legacy of that event has been anarchy. These dangers, says Mouchi, drove him and his family over the border in 2000. He now rents one of two cement structures on this stretch of land, which sets him apart from the others living under plastic sheets. And unlike those Gypsies, Mouchi has electricity and running water. Soon, however, he will be displaced, this time not by violence, but by a celebration of peace—the 2004 Olympic Games.

A new road being built for the Games will run through the Gypsy encampment. The city has condemned the land, and construction crews are scheduled to reach Mouchi's home in just two months. Already bulldozers have leveled half the field, mixing the dirt with the remains of shanties that stood on the land until days ago. Mouchi says he has no idea where his displaced compatriots went or where he will go when his time comes. He has money to pay for rent, he tells me, but it's difficult to find Greeks who will rent to Gypsies. He wishes the government would provide them with housing, perhaps some of those large metal shipping containers given to the country's most recent earthquake victims. "We, too, are human beings," he says. "We don't like living like this." By now, Mouchi's wife and their two other children have come to the sidewalk to see the stranger who has taken an interest in their lives. The wife is plump with a friendly smile. Both she and her husband have at least one gold tooth each. The daughter, who Mouchi says is six, looks older than that as she tends to her youngest brother, a toddler. When I ask about the children and school, Mouchi tells me that his daughter ought to go. He wants her to go. "Today, a person can't do anything without going to school," he says. But he adds that they will be in the area for only a few more months before they will have to move. It's now April; the school year is nearly over.

And so it goes for Gypsy children in Greece. The migratory lives of their parents either keep them out of school or disrupt their learning. Those who manage to make it to a classroom are more likely to learn about racism than reading and arithmetic. Teachers reportedly complain that Gypsy children are so unruly that they are impossible to teach, while Greek parents may not want Gypsies sharing the same classroom space as their children. Gypsy children who can overcome these problems must then master curricula geared toward native speakers of Greek, not Romany. And they must learn their lessons often without any help from their parents: for some 80 percent of the 300,000 Gypsies who live in Greece are illiterate.

Up the road, things are worse. Mouchi has agreed to take me into the shantytown. So we stride up the sidewalk, climb a mound of dirt and descend onto the field. Three teenage boys and a man, perhaps twice their age, are sitting on the ground. Nearby, a rusty barrel, cut in half and nailed to four wooden posts, holds some smoldering cinders that send a wisp of blue smoke into the twilight above. While I feel that we have just barged in, Mouchi takes an official tone and asks the others for their papers. "What?" he asks. "You don't have papers? You're all busted." I smile to try to put them at ease, but I am not successful. No Greek would voluntarily walk into the camp; each of us knows that. I get weary looks, although eventually the boys stare at me as if they have just spotted a celebrity. The man, however, remains reserved and distant, even afraid perhaps. There is a tension here that frightens me and has me wondering if Mouchi has just led me into a trap. But now my guide seems to be explaining my presence here and tells me that he will serve as my interpreter.

The man I am about to interview stands tall and has a dignified air about him. He is thin, but looks strong. A scraggly beard covers his leathery, dark face. Behind him there is only squalor. Four lopsided shacks built of wooden posts, plastic sheets, pieces of billboards, and cardboard boxes house him, his wife, and their eight children. Inside one of the shacks, women and children squat on dirty sheets spread over the dirt. There are no doors. I am tempted to use my camera, but the look in this man's proud face stops me. I sense that my presence here is making things more difficult, that the squalor is tolerable as long as no outsider sees it. But I am here, and I ask my questions. He and his oldest sons work as migrant farmworkers in central Greece for six months out of each year. During the other six, they come to Athens, where they survive by collecting metal cans, which they sell to a junkyard at two hundred drachmas, or about fifty cents, per kilogram. The three teenage boys now stand closer and they nod when the father talks about their work. One of the boys wears a rugby shirt with a New York Yankees logo. On this field, they have no running water, no electricity, and no sewage system. For water, they walk to a nearby faucet. They, too, have to leave the field soon. But because they are closer to the construction, their time here is shorter than Mouchi's. When I ask the father where he will take his family next, he shrugs and looks away.

I stand there feeling awkward and powerless. A little girl dashes by, running at full speed around one of the shanties.

When she notices me, she stops her game and stares at me, smiling. I tell the family patriarch that I wish there were a way I could help him. I extend my hand to him and he shakes it reluctantly. Soon I am back on the sidewalk, heading away.

The next few days are rainy and cold. I spend them in my room, thinking of life in the camp under the rain, of the children sleeping on the ground, and of my fears. I think that I have always known that this city holds so much misery. Perhaps everyone who lives here does. But I have not wanted to look for it; I have wanted to forget it and forget my share of it. Now it is taking all my strength to look. I wait for the rain to pass and plan my next expedition. This time I am headed to Zefyri, an area on the northwestern edge of the city and a large Gypsy enclave. A friend says the place has something of the Wild West, and I act nonchalant about the dangers.

Uncertain about how to get there, I board a bus headed to Ano Liossia, the northwest edge of the capital. Zefyri seems to be along the bus route, just south of the final destination. About twenty minutes from the center, the houses begin to grow apart and there are more trucks on the road. Here, near the edge, there is more sky. And things look all right as long as you keep your eyes skyward. On the ground, people are improvising at extending the city westward. New apartment buildings are going up next to shacks, car dealerships, and plots of farmland. Distance and space reduce the city to its essentials. The paving over of farmland and the opportunistic building spree so obvious here speak of the same anxiety to create housing that has driven Athens for the past fifty years. The bus crosses some railroad tracks that mark the city limits.

Nearby, a woman in a baseball cap tends a small herd of sheep. The urbanization of the rural landscape seems both crude and unstoppable.

Soon the bus pulls to a stop on an unpaved area at the side of the road. Outside the window, there is a bleak stretch of road, an active quarry, and little else. The two other passengers get off and I am left staring at the driver's back. "When is the next bus to Athens?" I ask him. "In about ten minutes," he says. "Is there a bus to Zefyri from here?" He tells me that I can ride this bus back to the railroad tracks and find my way on foot from there. He then steps outside for a smoke. I wait in my seat, watching trucks roll toward the quarry. Nascent apartment buildings and road construction crews await their return. From the city in the distance to the east, the hill yielding the stone blends in with the mountainous landscape. But from my westerly position, this hill is only the shell of a dusty, gaping hole. In the landscape to the south, I spot a cluster of buildings that make up Zefyri. The place looks to be a daunting five miles away over farmland and across a sprawling car cemetery. I have made it this far, but my resolve is now gone. When the bus sets off for the return trip, I decide that I will get off at the train tracks only if the driver remembers to notify me of the right stop. He never bothers to say a word, so I stay on, feeling ashamed and relieved.

At the final stop in central Athens, I ask the dispatcher if there is a bus that goes directly to Zefyri. "Why?" he asks me. "Do you need to get your fix?" Pleased with his wit, the dispatcher flashes a smile full of rotting teeth to a colleague standing nearby. I ignore the comment and hear the dispatcher give me the same directions as before: Get off at the railroad tracks and walk. "It's near," he says. "I know because I live there." He is the first person I meet who has been to Zefyri. "How are things there?" I ask him. The question sets the colleague and the dispatcher off. The colleague begins to tell me that things are wild there. "They all move about like Turks," he says. But the dispatcher is not going to sit by while his colleague bad-mouths his neighborhood, so he tries to reassure me that Zefyri is all right. The colleague, however, persists, saying that the dispatcher is defending the area only to avoid trouble from his savage neighbors. This last observation seems to strike the dispatcher, causing him to lose his temper. "Why?" asks the dispatcher, exasperated. "Are things any better in Kamatero?"—the colleague's neighborhood, which is just south of Zefyri. I leave them to sort out who lives in the more dangerous part of town.

The next day I try again. This time I have information directly from the government's transportation agency about a bus that stops right in Zefyri. I take the Metro to the bus, which comes right away. I make another bus connection, get off at the right stop, and ten minutes later I am on my way to Zefyri. I take this relative efficiency as a good omen. But as the bus heads northwest, the sky gets cloudy, and, near my destination, it starts to drizzle. By the time I get off, the rain is heavy. Now I am thinking that some higher force may be trying to warn me away from this place. I decide to wait out the rain inside the bus shelter. From here, the area looks like any of the working-class neighborhoods I have passed en route. Most of the houses are one- or two-story concrete blocks with balconies. But everywhere, there are new, taller apartment buildings in various states of completion.

To pass the time, I read the posters pasted to the bus shelter. The Greek Communist Party and the construction workers union are urging people to come out for the planned Labor Day rally on May 1. The communists' posters call for "solidarity, struggle, and mutual support in the fight against plutocracy and imperialism." Another poster condemns the "elasticity of labor relations," volunteerism, and the expectation that "We work for free for the good of the country and the [upcoming] Olympics." One can find these declarations almost everywhere in the city. But I imagine that their authors consider a marginal place like Zefyri especially promising in the recruitment of supporters. As I look at the new construction around me, at the effort people are making to emulate the middle class, I wonder if the message of class struggle really finds an audience here.

After a quarter of an hour, the downpour turns to drizzle. I try to ignore the lightning and thunder, and set out, leaving the protection of the bus shelter. At first, walking on the main road, I wonder what all the fuss was about. Zefyri does look poor and feel isolated, but the neighborhood is really no different from many others I have seen. There is a strip of stores—a small supermarket, a butcher, a jeweler, a place to bet on the soccer games—and a public square with a memorial to the student uprising of 1973. Here is also the legacy of the socialist government's twenty years in power and of the country's membership in the European Union. Zefyri's marginal status has attracted enough government funds to build four youth centers, a senior citizens' center, a "popular" theater, a municipal stadium, a nursery school, a public children's hospital, an elementary school, a junior high, and a high school. These sites—indicated on a map I carry with me—have a calming effect; Zefyri is not the wild place people described, but simply an area that's doing the best it can to offer its residents a decent standard of living.

But as I cross into the northern section of Zefyri, I become less sure of my assessment. Like railroad tracks elsewhere, here the city's new beltway forms a border between two parts of town. In the northern section, I can feel the difference and I don't like it. The neighborhood is nearly deserted, bereft of stores and passing cars. I find people again down a side street. Two men are plastering on the balcony of a bright white, brand-new two-story home. The house has a gaudy, festive look to it that makes it unlike any of the other new structures I have seen. The balustrades that encircle the second floor and the roof have much to do with this look. The balustrades are made up of a series of arcs, and the balusters are vaselike, adding so many curves to what is otherwise a concrete cube. There is a driveway on the side, and a wrought-iron fence all around the property. A couple of Gypsy children and women stand outside. Finally, I have found the Gypsies of Zefyri, about whom I have heard so much. Through the sliding glass doors of the ground floor, I catch a glimpse of a brand-new kitchen and dining area, but no furniture. The floor is strewn with toys and clothes that spill out onto the ground-floor patio. A Gypsy woman is moving around inside; another passes me on the street. I smile and say hello, using the formal address. "Are you selling something?" she asks me with great interest, which she loses as soon as I say "No." I am of no use to her, so she walks away.

These are Gypsies with disposable income and a fancy home, a combination I would have thought impossible just a minute before. And here is further evidence to counter the Greek misconception that Gypsies prefer to live out-of-doors and in filth. Given enough money and space, Gypsies will build large houses, just like any Greek. Money, however, is not enough to assimilate Gypsies into the Greek middle class. The difference that remains is that Gypsies are the victims of racism and Greeks are the perpetrators. It is no accident that this Gypsy family has built its home in this faraway outpost of Athens and not, say, near the Olympic Stadium. Land, of course, is cheaper in Zefyri, perhaps making a house like this affordable nowhere else for such a family. But the men plastering, the women and children moving about, the presence of this grand home in this desolate place—all exude a sense of freedom and entitlement that Gypsies could not attain in central Athens. Unburdened by the prejudice of neighbors, these people are making their lives proudly on the periphery.

On the block parallel to the one with the new house, a row of shacks restores the familiar image of Gypsies living in squalor. In the drizzle and thunder, this block looks miserable. Single-story cinder-block structures of varying heights line the street. Some of the roofs are held down with large rocks; all the roofs have television antennas. Out front, instead of a sidewalk there is a wide, unpaved strip that serves as a resting place for a few trucks, some decrepit lawn furniture, and trash. A couple of old Gypsy women with white headscarves stop to chat in the street. Two young girls walk by staring at me. I doubt any outsiders—any Greeks—have walked through here lately. My presence does not go unnoticed for long. When I am halfway down the street, I hear whistling and people calling out. A few moments pass before I realize that the sounds are directed at me. I turn to see a young Gypsy man gesturing at me to come over. He stands outside a crumbling shack with plastic sheets draping down from its roof. Elsewhere in Greece, the structure would probably pass for a chicken coop. I am too far away to speak, so I gesture back, asking what he wants. "We have," he calls out, and again he motions me to come close. Now instead of a potential seller, I have become a buyer. What else would a young Greek man be doing walking around here if not looking to score some drugs? The young man is trying to keep me interested while getting the attention of someone inside the shack. For a few moments, we stare at each other, about thirty meters apart. Soon, I know, more people will emerge from inside and things will get complicated. Without thinking, I raise my camera to one eye and shoot. The move convinces my solicitor that I am not here to buy. "Leave!" he yells. "Leave!" It looks to me as if he's going inside to warn the others. I oblige him.

On the main road again, I notice more homes like the brand-new one with the festive air. They all have the same architectural details: two stories with a balcony around the entire second floor, curved balustrades around the balcony, and decorative plasterwork. From each of the balconies hangs an escutcheon of sorts, which is round, blue with white fringes. These houses, like Gypsies themselves, stand out.

A Greek woman I meet at the bus stop tells me that she likes the new houses and that she is glad her neighbors are able to build them. The new construction, she says, is improving the area. She only complains about the "tent dwellers"— Gypsies who camp out-of-doors, creating hygiene problems for the area. She tells me that the local Gypsies who give these tent dwellers places to camp do not provide them with toilets. And then there is the drug trade, which she says is thriving. Gypsies and Greeks are involved, she tells me. Every morning on her way to work, she sees children strung out on drugs. "It's a shame," she says as we part ways.

As I wait for the bus back to central Athens, I think that Zefyri is wild, but not in the sense that people warned me about. By *wild*, they meant uncivilized, savage; it wasn't really the place they meant, but its residents. The distinction is important, because to brand the people as uncivilized is to overlook the prejudice and poverty at work here; it is to suggest that these Gypsies, all of these working-class residents, are somehow different from other Athenians. But it is Zefyri's social and economic marginality that invests the place with a sense of wildness. In such an environment, people break the rules: Gypsies build homes and people sell and buy drugs. Or, more to the point, they survive by emulating the same unfettered development and by adhering to the same market rules that shape the rest of this city. And that is truly wild.

BRIGHT NIGHTS

Her name is Maria, but she introduces herself to me as *Marie*, putting a hard accent on the *a*. The unusual twist is in keeping with a trend among women who take their Christian or ancient Greek appellations and tease out of them names that sound foreign. Marie is probably in her mid-thirties and has a sexy, weathered look, as if she has spent many late nights smoking and drinking in a place like this—Diogenis Studio.

The club is the sort that people here call *bouzoukia*, after the string instrument—the *bouzouki*—identified with Greek popular music. In such a place, there is a stage for the band, tables and chairs for the clubgoers, and maybe a dance floor. For the dancers, though, any flat surface will do, including the tabletops. A club, such as Diogenis Studio, will present the same show each night from late autumn until just before Easter. The club will then shut down for the summer, and the fun will move to clubs situated along the city's southern coast, the proximity to the sea lending a lighter, airy feel to nightly entertainment. It's now the middle of April, and the season at Diogenis Studio is coming to a close.

By 11:30 on a Thursday night, the club is full. Some two thousand people sit at rows of tables with maroon tablecloths, forming a semicircle around the stage, and wait for the show to start. Those who are less fortunate stand on the balcony. Everything is painted black, except for the wall around the club's interior perimeter. Here there are backlit, translucent orange panels that read VODAPHONE, the telecommunications company, and below the firm's name: HOW ARE YOU? Overhead, there are enough spotlights to light a Broadway play. Behind the bandstand, there is a silk screen of three illuminated red rosebuds that takes up the entire wall. Our table is right up against the front of the stage because we are with a big spender—a coarse twentysomething spending his father's money—who knows the manager. To get to our table, we have bypassed the people who are standing on line waiting to pay the standing-room charge, and walked past patrons at tables who look at us as if we must be important to be seated in such a prime spot. But while we are ahead of almost everyone in the place, we are not any more comfortable. Although Diogenis Studio is huge, there are so many tables and chairs squeezed into the place that everyone feels cramped. This is how I get to know Marie. Technically, she is sitting at the table next to ours, but she and I are so close that the distinction is meaningless.

To my eye, women outnumber the men. Ages range from late teens to late sixties. The women's hair color of choice is blond; everyone's favorite pastime is smoking. All the patrons are well dressed. Moments after we sit down, the standard fare arrives: bottles of Johnnie Walker Black, Coke, water, ice, and plates of fruit and dried nuts. A friend and government insider leans over and tells me that the building we are in was erected entirely with European Union funds. The late socialist prime minister, Andreas Papandreou, helped the owner, a close friend, secure the subsidy under the guise that the building would serve as a cultural center. It now houses a television studio and one other nightclub. Here, I think, is the socialists' revenge for decades of right-wing domination: putting the force of government at the service of popular culture, even if an evening here costs more than many Athenians make in a month.

Ten minutes after our arrival, we have run up a bill of about $700 or about as many euros. By opting to sit at a table, our party of six is obligated to buy at least two bottles of alcohol. The whiskey we order sells for about $200 a bottle. It is also customary at the *bouzoukia* to purchase white and red carnations, and then, in moments of glee, to toss them at the singers on stage. Each flower order comes in five shallow baskets for a total of $100. Women on staff, all wearing identical red dresses, stand in the aisles holding stacks of these baskets. A nod by the big spender summons three of the women, each of whom empties an order in the middle of our table. Later, when the small mound of carnations is gone, the women return. By the end of the night, the bill runs over $1,000. But because the big spender is a regular at Diogenis Studio, the manager reduces the total to about $600.

More than a gesture of goodwill, the reduction underscores an illusion cultivated at the *bouzoukia* that enjoyment and money are only loosely connected. Much is done to push the transaction of money for pleasure out of view. There are no menus, no price lists that I have ever seen; and at the end of the evening the waiter, or manager if you have consumed significantly, seems to calculate the grand total by sizing up the table rather than by adding a column of numbers. The outcome of the calculation is somewhat arbitrary, and if the bill is high, then the total becomes negotiable. The point of all this subterfuge is simple: At the *bouzoukia*, the constraints of the outside world disappear; one then enters a new realm, where the heart guides one's actions, not the mind. Emotions—and a limited number of them at that, consisting largely of passion, love, and heartbreak—outweigh rational considerations about money. At the *bouzoukia*, if all is done right, then the legendary figure of Zorba the Greek is brought to life. Given enough money, any clubgoer can become this prototypical modern Greek who, in his pursuit of a full and pleasurable life, disregards those of society's rules that stand in his way. Of course, that one can afford a night at Diogenis Studio is a fairly reliable indication that one adheres to these rules all too well.

Money is not only the conduit to Zorba's world, but also the catalyst of sexual interactions. A man who spends lavishly at the *bouzoukia* signals his income level and his willingness to spend money for his pleasure. With women around who are likely to respond to such signals, a man's money endows him with sexual potency. Dropping a thousand dollars on whiskey and carnations is akin to a mating call. For women, too, an extravagant night at the *bouzoukia* confuses sex and money. On the stage, or, better, on top of a table, a woman who moves her body to the erotic Eastern rhythms that make up much of Greek popular music puts a sexual side of herself on display. To her admirers, the message is not only that she does have such a side, but that she will bare it. And if you have enough money to come to Diogenis Studio, then you can afford to see it.

I have little money, but, by association with the big spender, I become one of the men who have enough wealth to be paid attention to. I sense the power of my enhanced status as the people at Marie's table watch the easy and careless way with which expensive whiskey and pricey, odorless carnations fill our table. Sharing in the big spender's glow, I strike up a conversation with Marie. I think it quickly becomes clear to her that I am not the big-spending type. It's my first time here (she comes here often); I live in the indistinct section of Koukaki; I don't have a car. Still, I offer up enough glamorous-sounding bits—a writer from New York, a former journalist—that I sustain the flirtation. We spend four hours occasionally sharing information about ourselves, telling each other if we like the next song, and smelling each other's hair as we lean in to be heard over the loud music.

In the show's first hour, several women and one man take turns singing small sets to warm up the crowd, which largely ignores them. The repertoire ranges from Greek pop songs to American disco and soul. Two women, one black and one white, specialize in '70s disco hits and unimpressive renditions of "Respect" and "Soul Man." There are also elaborate stage effects, including a bandstand that disappears into the stage floor as another descends from the ceiling. I know I am in Athens, but it feels like Las Vegas.

At 12:40 a.m., the first and the younger of the two headliners, Antonis Remos, walks on. In the narrow aisles between tables, the club's flower women stand at the ready. They all wear the same dress and hold stacks of the shallow flower baskets. With a quick nod, the big spender summons two of the women, and they empty their baskets on our table. The scene is repeated over and over again throughout the evening at the tables near the stage. When Remos leans into the microphone, the carnations start to fly. Those who are really taken by the performance send the flower women directly to the stage to empty their baskets at his feet. Sometimes the women will relay a secret message from the wealthy patron to the performer as they dump the flowers, or they will simply point in the direction of the table that is adding to its bill. As he sings his first song, Remos walks around the stage nodding and winking at select members of the clientele. In between verses of his first song, he exchanges a few words with someone here, shares an inside joke with someone there. For the young heir of a corrugated-cardboard fortune at our table, Remos reserves a special treat. The singer greets him by name, using the microphone. The big spender responds by throwing a fistful of carnations toward the stage. Remos will repeatedly acknowledge the moneyed young man, eliciting the same response each time.

Song after song is about heartbreak, betrayal, and everlasting love. For the crowd, each song seems to evoke a personal history. The people around me sing along, applaud, and toast one another, as if the lyrics bring to mind old wounds, as if the songs were written just for them. But here, tonight, memory will be exorcised. We will sing, drink, and leave our troubles strewn around the stage like so many withering carnations. This all happens, however, according to a standard code of celebration that makes the experience seem staged and trite. When a hit song is performed, for example, each member of the audience will sing along and lift one hand in the air, keeping the palm open and sideways, and bend the arm at the elbow to the rhythm of the music. The gesture is straight out of Greek music videos, but it has become so integral to what clubgoers do that it is now difficult to tell whether people are fulfilling an image of themselves they have learned from television, or if they created the image in the first place. Either way, the gesture is so common, so familiar, that it comes off as self-conscious; this is what you do if the song speaks to you. The code also prescribes a limited range of other behaviors: the flower tossing, a variation of belly dancing by the women, a drunkenlike solo dance by the men (and increasingly by women), and the consumption of hard alcohol. The *bouzoukia*, it seems to me, promise the clubgoer entrée into the mythical world of Zorba, where there is ecstasy in liberation. But imagining Athenians going through this familiar set of motions night after night and in club after club leaves me wondering if that promise is ever fulfilled.

Sometime after two in the morning, the other headliner, Iannis Parios, the evening's really big name, walks on stage. For the next hour and a half, Parios, either alone or with Remos, sings recent hits and old favorites. The bandstand rises to reveal a second group of musicians underneath, while Parios exits, only to reappear moments later in a new outfit on a platform that emerges from the stage floor. The songs are singlemindedly about love. Outside of the joy or pain of love, nothing else seems worth singing about. For some forty years, Parios has had tremendous success with the love-song genre. Throughout times of war, political violence, and economic struggle, he has continued to record hit after hit about that one and only woman walking in or out of his life. It is startling to me, then, to see an image of Mikis Theodorakis—the country's quintessential political composer—suddenly projected on the wall that previously held the illuminated rosebuds. The lights dim, the club becomes quiet, and Parios now looks serious. No, the show is not about to turn political and the audience knows it. Parios is simply poised to perform some of the composer's love songs, as he has done on a recent recording. Still, Theodorakis's virtual presence has a sobering effect. But I sense that the mood change stems not from the political struggles for democratic rule that the composer invokes, but from a vague sense of embarrassment, or perhaps aversion, as the reality of the outside world encroaches on the club's fantasy. Perhaps Parios is aware of this effect, but I don't think he can resist the temptation to link himself with Theodorakis. For decades, the composer has been identified with political struggle and his music has energized the fight for democracy in countries around the world. Parios, too, has been widely popular, but in a different, less revered way. He will be remembered for having sung love songs, not for inspiring the nation with his art. And Parios's move to record Theodorakis's love songs, so late in his career, when his singing skills have precipitously declined, seems to me an effort to somehow enhance this legacy by association. The slide show behind Parios clearly evokes Theodorakis's legendary status, portraying the composer's disembodied profile over a black background. But now Parios shares this elevated status: The singer's profile has been added to suggest that here we have two legends, not one, gazing intently at something in the distance. We are led to believe that while one man sang about love and the other wrote the music of revolutions, all along both were focused on the same unnamed and elusive goal. The image, of course, is doctored.

> My father spends hours in the evenings and weekends sitting at the kitchen table, crouched next to his cassette player and the small stacks of tapes he makes. Every so often he will ask me to listen to a song he is just now recording, but I never seem able to show him that I appreciate it enough. Still, by the time I am ten, I know the refrains of some of Parios's songs, and I sing them to myself on the way to school. I know the name *Theodorakis*, too, but not much else.

By now, Marie and I are sharing personal but vague information about our lives, having reached a level of comfort with each other that opens the way for small intimacies. What's my sign? We're both Capricorns. I tell her I am single; she tells me that she is seeing someone, a fact that intensifies our flirting by making it almost explicitly sexual. To savor the intensity, I ask her if she loves him. They get along, she says, but "falling in love, at this stage in my life, if it were to fail, would jeopardize many of the things that I have created for myself." "Is there true love?" I ask. "A man should love a woman," she says. I try to point to the irony of taking such a cynical view while spending an evening listening and singing along to songs about love, but somehow I fail to make my point, so I drop it. A little before four in the morning, she takes my number and gets up to go. As she walks away, she pushes a couple of carnations into my hand. This will be the last time I see her.

At 4 a.m., Parios is done, and now it's time to dance. The younger Remos takes over, singing old songs that are dance favorites. Young men and women flood the stage, to alternate between dancing the Greek version of the belly dance (*tsifteteli*) and *zeimbekikos*, a traditionally male dance that is supposed to convey a sense of pain. Any pain exhibited here though is feigned, the dancing more an opportunity for fun than an expression of heartfelt angst. By 4:30 a.m., we, too, are done, although the show goes on. Most of the patrons are still at their tables. It's now Friday morning. A young woman in our group—a schoolteacher—says she has to get up at seven to go to work.

It's at least an hour before dawn, the dark making the transition to the outside easier. Soon a friend drops me off and I watch his BMW speed away down the empty boulevard. The young teacher keeps him company on the ride home. I cannot hear it, but I know he has the radio on and that it is playing one of the songs we heard tonight.

6   ON SUNDAY

My primer from 1975 opens with a section titled "Images for Oral Instruction," which is composed of three wordless illustrations—the family sitting in its living room, the family going to church, and the family's two oldest children performing in a school play about Greek independence. By the time the new stock of first graders arrived in schools that September, the government had had time to purge books of the deposed junta's emblem, showing a soldier, a phoenix, and a flame. But the junta's cherished model of Greek society, rooted in the life of the family, in religion, and in nationalism, was still there, just as potent for the current democratic government as for the dictators before them. Our education would begin the very first day on a preliterate level with images that were to reinforce, or more likely to imprint, the fundamental constructs of our world on our young psyches. In the weeks and months ahead, these same ideas of family, Christianity, and love of country would form the subtext of learning to read. Church bells, for example, taught me how to read the Greek combination of the letters *nu* and *tau* that make the sound *d*. "Ding dong, ding dong, the bell is ringing" reads this lesson. "Today is Sunday."

While we were supposed to learn that family, religion, and the state were to sustain us all the time, Sunday held a special position in this pedagogical fantasy, not because it was the one day when parents, or at least fathers, did not have to work, and children did not have to attend school—which would have been to acknowledge the pressures of the real world—but because it was the day to go to church. On this day and in that place, these social constructs fused into a harmonious and inseparable whole. Here was the family together, worshipping Christ, and ostensibly listening to the priest end the Divine Liturgy with prayers for the nation and its armed forces. And while neither my family nor any other families I knew went to church on Sundays, I never remember being bothered by this discrepancy between what was and what was supposed to be.

Of all the schoolbooks I ever had, I remember only this primer. And I am not alone. While the book was withdrawn from schools after a few years, a reprinted edition is now sold by street vendors around Athens. This popularity, I think, has to do with the book's success in drawing its young readers and perhaps their parents into a world that felt safe, made up of the pleasures of childhood, and shaped by nature and tradition. In this world, the children celebrate "the gifts of the sun," they sing songs about the flag, and they say their prayers each night before going to bed. Of course, none of us would have been drawn into this idyllic realm, or would now feel nostalgic enough to buy a reissued copy of the primer, were this world not so different from our own.

During the months that I spend in Athens, the church bells do ring each Sunday morning. But for those who can make it to church by eight in the morning, hoping for entry into the realm of God, family, and country, the experience disappoints. In my primer, church was the place the family hurries to on Sunday mornings, and where the priest is a kindly old man who knows all the children by name. The family's elderly grandmother is never shown accompanying the others to church; on Easter night, we learn that she stays at home, ostensibly because she's too old to walk around. However, on the Sunday mornings that I make it to the different churches around Athens, I am usually the only person in the congregation under retirement age. And while few families are ever here, God and country are. But they, too, seem different, devoid of the power to inspire and comfort that figured so large in my primer.

When I walk into my first liturgy at 8:30 on a pleasant Sunday morning, it's been years since I've been to church, but you wouldn't know it. Without effort, I begin to move in the ritualized ways ingrained in me on so many school trips to the neighborhood church. Then as now, the first priority was to avoid drawing attention to oneself. So I bow and kiss the icons to the left and to the right of the entrance, I do not speak, I make the sign of the cross, stay out of the center aisle, and take my seat among the men on the right side of the cavernous room. My age makes me stand out in this gray-hair crowd, but having done everything as I am supposed to, I blend in without incident. The only difficulty, I soon realize, remains a lack of decisiveness about whether to sit or remain standing. I try to take cues from the people around me, but all I get are mixed signals. I am not the only one who is confused. I see men more than twice my age starting to sit but catching themselves before their posteriors hit the pews. About an hour into the service, I realize that it's good to stand and remain standing when the priest is chanting or when he appears at the entrance to the altar; and it's okay to sit (sometimes) when the choir sings filler prayers in between.

What I failed to learn from my school days both in church and in religion classes is what the priest says during the service. Sure I get highlights: the Our Father (*Pater Imon*), the prayer one says as one makes the sign of the cross. But that the liturgy is said in an older Greek dialect and that it is chanted prevents me from understanding. When I was younger, I always thought the problem stemmed from my parents' failure to send me to Sunday school. Later I figured that few really understand much of what's being said. Only the black-clad, octogenarian faithful, who have heard the liturgy repeated countless times and who pensively mouth some of the chants, seem to have an insight into what's happening. The rest of us, I have always felt, sit there mystified solely out of a sense of obligation, which in this Greek Orthodox country is rarefied into tradition and eventually transfigured into faith. The obfuscating process begins a year or so after birth, when infants are officially given their names and welcomed into God's realm at their baptism—a ritual whose mythical power to transform long ago gave way to concerns about hiring the right caterer. And the process continues well after death with memorial services at prescribed times—nine and then forty days after one's passing. Skip either one and risk the censure of your friends and neighbors for having neglected the deceased. In between birth and death, either the Church or the State is likely to get you again with mandatory religion classes in school, or if you decide to get married. Only young people, and those for whom resisting obligation is still important, seem to escape this ecclesiastical domination, if only temporarily.

With the liturgy nearing its end, parents taking their children to receive communion have shown up. One father takes a plastic comb out of his back pocket and runs it one last time through his young son's hair. A mother holds a toddler in a pink satin dress. The old men and women, who will receive communion (a mix of sweet, warm wine and bread) from the same spoon as the children, stand at the back of the line. But they must wait a little longer. On this day, the priest interrupts the service to read a long-winded announcement issued by the Holy Synod of the Church of Greece about the upcoming Olympics. The Church is determined, we are told, to contribute to the successful attainment of this national goal by organizing cultural events that will promote the country's heritage, which is by definition Christian. The Holy Synod is also exhorting young and able members of the laity to volunteer as hosts and guides during the games. Those who are interested, says the priest, can pick up volunteer application forms in the church office. I am guessing he hopes that the grandparents in attendance will inform their grandchildren. When the service resumes, those who have fasted move forward to receive communion. The rest of us wait in our seats. When that ritual is completed, the priest appears at the entrance to the altar for a final prayer that asks God to bless, among others, the faith, the nation, and the armed forces. At 10 a.m., smileless, he bids us *"Kalimera," or "Good day."* The parishioners exit quickly, most of them stepping over the couple of beggars who have convened at the steps of the church.

The following Sunday, again I set out for church but decide to change locations, hoping for a warmer and more inspiring experience. At 8:30 in the morning, a handful of older men and women sit at the pews of a small church in Plaka, the women on the left, the men on the right. Over the next two hours, a few more people trickle in, among them some younger parents and their children. I spend the time trying to lose myself in the spiritual atmosphere created by the chanting, the burning frankincense, and the stern faces on the icons. I remain standing for as long as I can, using the discomfort in my legs as a focus for my meditation. In the ritual going on around me, I look for meaning, but I am often distracted from my search by the ritual itself. I see the priest performing the precise movements that the service dictates, the old women who kneel before and kiss the icons in the same sequence, the men who stand every time the priest shows up at the entrance to the altar. All seem like gestures motivated by obligation and habit, symbolic acts whose meaning has long since been forgotten. In the midst of it all, one woman goes around with a bottle of blue glass cleaner, spraying and wiping the kiss marks off the glass that protects the icons.

This priest is far younger than most of his parishioners. He has curly hair and a beard trimmed so short that it makes him look trendy. His age and his contemporary look make me hopeful that he will inject something new into the ritual, a trace of something invigorating. But like his older colleagues elsewhere, he goes through two hours barely looking at those assembled before him. He moves mechanically as if he disdains us. Even during his sermon, he never looks at any of us. Instead, he keeps his eyes focused someplace around the exit of the church. But then he surprises me. He sermonizes about Christ, who he says reveals to us the Word of God. The Word of God is in everything that exists. And all of us, he says, according to our spiritual ability, may come to learn something of this power that is in us, that is in everything. His manner throughout the liturgy has suggested that he does not think much of our spiritual ability, but here he's offering something potentially radical—namely, that God is not someplace up above, monitoring and passing judgment on the world, but that each of us has something of the divine within us. I look around for some visible effect this notion has on the people around me, but find none. The priest's mechanical, rushed delivery, too, suggests that our chances of understanding the meaning of his words are slim. He wraps up quickly and returns to the prescribed activities of ritual: communion, the passing of the bread, a final blessing. He then bids us *"Kalimera,"* turning hurriedly toward the altar and doffing his hat all in one motion. I linger around outside, watching the men and women of the congregation greet one another and ignore the Gypsy women who are panhandling.

On Sundays we always eat meat and pasta. Today, three chunks of pot-roasted beef sit on top of a heaping plate of spaghetti. By the amount of food, it's easy to tell that this is my father's plate even before my mother sets it in front of him. But it is not as easy to tell which plate is mine and which belongs to her. My first impulse is to assume that, as the youngest, the smallest portion is mine. I am wrong. We eat to the breathless radio broadcast of soccer games coming out of a little radio sitting on top of the kitchen table.

If the authors of that old primer of mine wanted to put some real-world muscle behind their pedagogical notions of family, national unity, and faith, they would have done much better showing the family attending a soccer match. For, while on paper Sunday was devoted to church, it has been soccer that has been synonymous with God's day for as long as I can remember. The sport makes a single brief appearance in the primer when the family's son is shown kicking a ball while on a trip to the country. In real life, however, boys played soccer all the time, our fathers listened, watched, read about, and wagered on the games religiously, and everyone who was not female argued on Monday morning about their favorite teams' performances the day before. To this day, men meeting for the first time will often try to make small talk by asking each other, What team are you? The wrong answer can elicit an earful from your cabdriver, or an argument from a person you just met. Team identity engenders in fans a sense of devotion, energy, and passion that both the Church and the State must envy. In this calculus, the team is everything for its fans—a

more potent signifier and a more tangible signified for cama-
raderie, loyalty, and inspiration than God and country. "PAO-
Religion" is a favorite slogan among fans of an Athenian team
with that acronym, but soccer is a religion of sorts for every
fan here.

In this horribly congested city, where apartment buildings
rise high above narrow streets and where open space is a luxury, Athenians have found myriad ways to squeeze soccer
fields into the urban landscape. I find soccer fields in the midst
of private homes, but also in the bed of a dried pond in the
section of Nea Penteli, and, my favorite, on the floor of an
abandoned quarry in Kallithea. The neighborhood's name
means "good view," but that must be a moniker from another
time. From the road that circles the field, I can see only old
apartments that are baking in the hot sun. I follow the road in
search of the stadium entrance, but wind up in a dump for car
parts. The excavated stone of the quarry is visible from here,
but not the entrance. I climb the little streets around the rocky
hill and manage to find another dead end, a lemon tree, and a
barking dog. I retreat, climb higher, and finally make it to the
top of the hill. From a schoolyard full of graffiti, I can see the
field below: green grass, a red track, and the old quarry everywhere. There is a strange beauty here—the green field in the
broken rock, wildflowers growing in the crevices. Two-thirds
of the hill has been chewed away and spat back to make the
apartment buildings all around. But that was the work of the
past. Now the neighborhood's second-tier team plays soccer
in the hill's cavernous belly. A working-class stadium for a
working-class neighborhood, and a team that will never be
great but takes the field every Sunday nonetheless.

Olympiakos (Olympic) is everything that the Kallithea soccer team is not—the country's richest and most successful club.
With a handful of games left in the regular season of the
A-Division, Olympiakos trails its cross-town rival, AEK, by
one point. In division play, there are no playoffs to determine
the winner. Finish in first place and you win the Championship, as well as entrée into Europe's Champions League—a
tournament of the continent's top teams. And winning is rewarded with cash. By scoring points in the Champions League,
for example, a team gets bonuses from UEFA (Union des Asso-
ciations Européennes de Football), the organization that gov-
erns soccer in Europe. A winning team, such as Olympiakos,
also commands television contracts that are a great deal more
lucrative than those negotiated by most of its Greek competition, and enjoys far more marketing opportunities for its
merchandise than the teams it regularly beats on Sundays.
Olympiakos, AEK, and a third Athenian team, Panathinaikos
(Pan-Athenian), tend to dominate divisional play. Olympiakos,
for instance, has won thirty Championships, twenty Cups, two
Super Cups, and one Balkan Cup in the first seventy-five years
of its history, or nearly one major title each year. That sort of
success helps perpetuate a system in which the richest teams
are rewarded with the largest cash infusions, enabling them to
afford the best players, while most of the other teams in the
division wallow in mediocrity, beaten week after week by the
top three or four clubs. The less successful clubs also operate
as unofficial farm teams for the division leaders; they develop
young, talented players, whose playing rights they then sell to
successful franchises such as Olympiakos.

Growing up with a father who settled for listening to soccer matches on radio rather than risk the violence of the stadium or pay the price of admission, I attend my first soccer match on a crisp Sunday afternoon in April, at the age of thirty-two. Today Olympiakos takes on a little-known team, Akratitos (Unrestrained), which is playing in the A-Division for the first time in its thirty-eight-year history. Everything about this matchup suggests that the game will be an easy one for the defending champions. Olympiakos has once again been dominant in divisional play, the team has the better players (mostly non-Greeks from other parts of Europe, Africa, and South America), superior training facilities, and the home-field advantage. That Akratitos is based in Ano Liossia, a poor neighborhood known for its Gypsy population and the city's garbage dump, makes the disparity between these two teams even greater. The difference, of course, has to do with money. A printed program for the game informs the reader that Akratitos's total capitalization amounts to 200 million drachma, or about half a million dollars. The program doesn't offer a comparable figure for Olympiakos, but we all know that Akratitos's total worth is only a fraction of the home team's payroll.

Assured of victory, the fans of the home team are strolling toward the city's Olympic Stadium, a sprawling and worn athletic complex near the posh northern suburbs. Here, as in most places where soccer is played around the world, the sport is tinged with violence. But there is so little at stake in this game, the result so predictable, that tensions are low and the police presence is minimal. The only hint of violence comes from the vendors who line the walkways leading to the stadium. They urge the passing crowd to spend their pocket change on foul-looking souvlakis, sausages, and nuts by shouting that the cops are confiscating all coins at the stadium entrances. Pelting the game officials, rival fans, and players with coins has become a last resort of impassioned fans forbidden from bringing other weapons to games. When we reach the stadium, ticket takers rip our tickets along the perforation. They return one portion to us; their part they toss on the ground. Next, a cop half-heartedly pats down my coat pockets and feels something hard. I tell him it is a small camera and he waves me on.

I have come expecting violence, but once inside the atmosphere is hardly tense. The mostly male crowd sits around smoking and sipping cold instant coffee through straws. Some fathers have brought their sons; a few of the men have come with their wives and girlfriends. A priest arrives. A boy unwraps his lunch on his lap: a piece of spanakopita. One section away, the red seats of the VIP section fill. For the very very important persons, there are a few rows of high-backed brown leather armchairs, the kind you might find in an old library. Only the hard-core fans, confined to one section at the opposite side of the stadium, sustain the potential for violence. A few thousand of them chant, move, and clap in unison, exuding a violent energy that only a frenzied crowd can muster. But with victory all but guaranteed, the obscene chants and paeans to Olympiakos emanating from that section seem more like a self-gratifying ritual than preparation for battle. The stadium officials further undercut any tension that has built up before the start of the game by blaring the home team's hokey theme song over the public address system. There is no playing of the national anthem here, nor any Greek flags that I can see. Loyalty here begins and ends with Olympiakos. One giant banner put up by fans from the town of Argos, who customarily occupy the section near the stadium's gate 7, reads: ARGOS 7: WE ARE READY TO DIE FOR YOU.

Olympiakos quickly scores first, drawing a burst of excitement from the fans. But the exuberance is short-lived. Akratitos stuns the crowd by tying the score. From now on, the fans sit and watch intently, looking more like they are listening to a lecture than watching a game. I am rooting for the underdogs, but I judge that it's safer to keep this sentiment to myself. The tension in the stands builds as the time ticks away and Olympiakos's play gets sloppier. Whenever the home team makes a mistake, the fans disparage its coach and players with expletives that make me wonder why anyone would bring a child here. Then Akratitos does the unthinkable: It takes the lead. The men around me looked shocked, disgusted, and then angry. Watching the players of Akratitos celebrate, one fan wonders aloud about the dark complexion of the visitors. "They're all Gypsies," he says. Olympiakos has missed several scoring opportunities and finally does manage to score before the game ends. But the tie score has cost Olympiakos valuable points in the competition for the Championship.

Conditions are raunchier and more volatile the next week, when I attend an AEK home game in the Nea (new) Philadelphia section of Athens. Greek refugees fleeing back to Greece from Turkey in the 1920s started their lives over in this area, and gave the neighborhood a name to reflect their refugee status. (Philadelphia is the ancient Greek name for the Turkish town of Alasehir.) Their soccer team, AEK, the Greek acronym for "Athletic Union of Constantinople," would remind them of their displacement and unite them in their struggle to start fresh. A black two-headed eagle, looking both east and west, on a bright yellow background—the emblem of the Byzantine Empire—would serve as the team logo. Now it would be up to this soccer team to carry on the glory of a time long gone. That decades later AEK fans would drive from all over Athens to see their team play was apparently not foreseen by the club's founders, who neglected to build a parking lot around the stadium. So on game day, the neighborhood is clogged with cars, forcing fans to park blocks away and walk. A friend and I park illegally and follow the crowd that makes its way through the narrow streets and low apartment buildings that are built right next to the stadium. AEK is one of the country's most successful teams and a contender on the European level, but from here its presence feels like just another part of the neighborhood, proximate and modest.

We make our way through a chaotic mass of fans, street vendors, and cops, looking for the ticket windows. Instead, we find three yellow booths that look like they once served as portable toilets. Around each, a crowd of men jostles each other to get to the window. Inside, women sit in darkness, pulling in cash and pushing tickets out. A vendor peddling Styrofoam seat cushions convinces us that the seats inside are filthy (it turns out that he is right) and then we head to the entrance. A police officer asks me to empty one of my many pockets, and lets me pass when I show him its contents. Atop the drab cement structure that forms this stadium fly three flags: Greece's, AEK's, and Nike's—a white swoosh on a black background. The dome and cross of a neighboring church peeks over the stadium walls. And across from where we are sitting, a large sign reads IMMORTAL BYZANTIUM. But while the people here may have refused to let the memory of that empire die, they have not shown the same resolve in maintaining anything else in the stadium. The field looks green, but its grass seems sparse and atrophied. Around it is the sorriest track you've ever seen. Only a lone gardener seems to be battling the misery of the place, planting a few rosebushes behind one of the goalposts. But nobody seems to care. Fans curse, sing, bang, jump, jostle, and chant. And the old stadium proves a fitting crucible for it all.

The rowdiest of the fanatics occupy one of the far ends of the stadium. A tall wire fence that rises in front of them is supposed to prevent these rabid fans from jumping into the field or throwing things at the players. But caging them in and leaving them unattended just makes them wilder, since the fence creates a separate space where anything goes. Stadium officials seem to like it that way, because, apart from ticket revenue, these fans represent a force that the team owner can mobilize to serve his needs. In Greece, where government regulates and subsidizes soccer, and where the diversified business interests of team owners can depend on the favor of the governing administration, having a legion of crazed fans at your disposal makes political sense. A few inflammatory words from the team owner and these fanatics can turn into a small army ready to riot, take on the police, destabilize the city, and discredit the government. So instead of trying to control these fans, the stadium officials egg them on. At the start of each half, a field crew sets off canisters that spew out orange smoke in front of this section, making it look more like a street battle than an athletic competition. When AEK scores, young fans jump high onto the fence and rock it back and forth, while flares stream over it and into the field. These antics draw a reaction from neither the police nor stadium officials.

In response to this official permissiveness, the fanatics infuse the stadium with an almost intoxicating euphoria. They sing and dance in unison and lead everybody else in chants that sometimes glorify their team, and sometimes disparage not the visiting team, but AEK's only real competitor for the Championship, Olympiakos. Each chant is accompanied by a different gesture or clapping sequence. Some are playful, some are threatening. But there is one that is unlike any of the others. When AEK blows the game open by taking a three-to-nothing lead, fans everywhere stand, raising one hand above their heads. With the palm open and turned sideways, they slice the air in time with their chant: "There-there-there-go-the-champions." The spectacle is straight out of a Nazi rally. Flares go off in the hard-core section, with some making it over the fence and falling onto the track. Crews pick them up, still flaring, and toss them away from the field. The sparks set a banner on fire, while the players of the visiting team, Iraklis (Hercules), look around as if they are trapped.

AEK's victory in this game and another by Olympiakos mean that the Championship winner will be decided in a head-to-head match between the two division leaders in just six days. With so much at stake, the meeting between the two teams promises to be less a game and more a showdown between rival tribes. So on game day, the police prepare for a battle. Trains reserved for Olympiakos fans only transport them from Piraeus—the team's traditional lair—to the Olympic Stadium. To prevent skirmishes with AEK fans along the way, cops in riot gear are stationed at each of the stations through which these trains pass. Once the faithful reach the stadium, police try to keep the fans of each team far apart by escorting them into the stadium through separate paths and entrances.

I arrive on the back of a friend's motorcycle with special invitations to the stadium's press section, not because I am a journalist, but because I have another friend whose father is an important politician. Our passes give us access to a smoky reception area with what appears to be the stadium's only concession stand. The room is packed with people who, like me, got free tickets because they know someone who knows someone else. The space seems to exist not to serve journalists covering the game, but to accommodate the ubiquitous exchange of favors. Sooner or later, everyone takes turns being either a patron or a client; it is how anything of consequence gets done here. What do you want? A job? A contract? An official document? An operation? To get into a club? To spare your son the hardship of military service? Anything is possible if you have the right connection, or what Greeks alternatively call "medium," "plug," or "tooth." Today it is Olympiakos doling out the free passes; tomorrow it may be one of us who will be asked to help the team owner, to write something positive for the team, or just to ignore the violent insanity that surrounds the sport. In the meantime, we can choose from one of three types of Scotch whiskey at the concession stand—no need to wait on line.

In the stands, a battle is brewing. AEK fans have been relegated to one of the far ends of the stadium, and the sections on either side have been left empty. In these dividing spaces, riot police stand in green military overalls and helmets, holding clubs and shields. All around are Olympiakos fans, chanting and clapping themselves into a frenzy. There is a chant to the tune of "Jingle Bells" and another that parodies the Greek national anthem. And there are less imaginative ones, such as one that depends simply on rhyme. Some fans call out "double-headed eagle"—a nickname for AEK—and others answer: "whore's son." When fans are not insulting each other, they threaten the referee's life, disparage the coaches, and curse at the players for making mistakes. Occasionally, a flare will streak across the evening sky and land among the AEK fans. Someone there will then pick it up and hurl it back. When one of the teams scores, the firing of flares turns into a barrage, while the cops just stand there like overwhelmed animal trainers.

No serious incidents of violence are reported that night. Anyone reading a newspaper account the next morning would learn of a spirited game in which Olympiakos edged AEK by a score of 4–3. The legendary team added another title to its storied record. AEK fought valiantly but lost. And everything was as it should be in Athens. The game was played on a Saturday night, but it might as well have been Sunday.

EASTER

In the twentieth century, the Greek countryside was largely vacated. Every Easter, however, the people return. And for a few days, it is Athens' turn to be abandoned.

Immigration to the United States and elsewhere first offered a way out of the hard life of subsistence farming in the 1890s. In the next one hundred years, those who did not travel abroad usually opted to emigrate to Greek cities—Thessosloniki, Patras, and especially Athens. If it was not the promise of a better-paying job that drove villagers to the cities, then it was war, political persecution, and the lack of educational opportunity. The capital became the most lucrative destination because both industry and government services were concentrated here. Now out of a Greek population of some 10 million, nearly half live in Athens.

People who have spent most of their lives in the city still say they come from someplace else. Athens is a place to put up with while one makes a living. But one's hometown is a source of identity and pride; it's a place where life was difficult, but where things were simpler and more pure. This sense of belonging someplace else is so dominant that even those who are born in Athens often cannot claim an urban origin. As a child of internal immigrants, I learned to tell people that I was "born in Athens," instead of saying that I was from Athens. The distinction signals that I am not really an Athenian, that my connection to the capital reflects only the vagaries of fate that landed my parents here. (For my mother it was the earthquake of 1953 on the island of Cephalonia that first brought her to Athens; for my father, it was the nationalism of Egypt's Gamal Abdel Nasser that uprooted him from Cairo—once a popular destination of Greek immigration.) Telling someone that I was born here inevitably elicits the next question: "Where is your father from?" In my case, even the answer to that question is complicated, since my father was born outside Greece. To satisfy my questioner, I must trace my true origin back to my paternal grandfather, who is from the island of Samos.

On Easter, Athenians cut through such tangled personal histories of emigration by heading back to their villages. Since my arrival in April, I have received three invitations from friends and relatives to join them for the trip out of the city in early May. To these people, staying in the capital over the holiday seems ludicrous, or at least unfortunate. By Holy

Thursday, I see what they mean. Signs in the windows of shops announce that the stores will reopen in a week. If one forgets to do one's shopping ahead of time, then one has two options: Either live on pastries, since pastry shops are the only stores that remain open through much of the holiday, or starve. There are fewer people walking the streets, fewer cars. To stay in town, no doubt, is to feel left behind.

My trip out of town begins at 6 a.m. on Good Friday. I have accepted an invitation from my cousin and her family for a trip to her husband's parents' village outside the city of Volos, 330 kilometers north of Athens. The plan is to beat traffic by leaving early. Others walking the streets with duffel bags at that early hour apparently have the same plan. By 7:30 a.m., a small sport utility vehicle is loaded with our luggage, my cousin, her husband Michalis, their three young daughters, and me. For about an hour, traffic moves well along the four-lane highway heading north. But then an accident slows traffic to a crawl. We do not speak about the crash because we all know what each other is thinking. On such holiday weekends, Greek highways turn into a bloodbath. The highway we are on makes it easy to see why, as it suddenly narrows to a single lane. Now to pass a slow-moving truck, or a farmer who has decided to take his tractor out for a spin, drivers veer into on-coming traffic. Coming around a bend in the road, one such driver comes recklessly close to hitting us. Add drunk driving and a dearth of traffic signs to the poor road design, and the casualties mount. Between Holy Thursday and the Monday af-ter Easter, the police will report that 39 people were killed and 280 injured in 205 auto accidents. Death, the village, city life—these are the undercurrents of our trip, of every Athenian on the road today. But as we drive on, we keep these ideas separate, as everyone does to keep going.

After five hot hours in the car, we finally arrive at the village of Agria, outside of Volos. The village sits at the foot of Mount Pelion, the mythic playground of the god Pan: the half-man, half-goat who frolicked in the company of nymphs. By the late afternoon, Michalis and I find ourselves in a pastoral landscape where the hoofed deity would fit right in. A short car ride from his parents' home brings us to an olive grove, where his father has set up his own private playground. Many years past retirement, the old but sturdy man comes here to pass the time among a small herd of goats and sheep, a ferocious dog, and some chickens. Four shacks, made of scrap wood, sheets of tin, and salvaged shingles, stand at the highest point of this sloped field. The largest one, with an area of just a few square meters, serves as a place for the father to rest, to eat a simple lunch, to take shelter from the rain. Everything in the room speaks of a life working the earth. On the dirt-packed floor, there is a cot, a refrigerator, a table, and a wicker chair. Nothing is new and everything is in its place. Rusty tools, dented pots and pans, and plastic soda bottles filled with oil and wine crowd the shelves and countertops. The low ceiling holds everything else for which there is no room on the floor or the shelves: a scale, a long row of sheep bells, and bags of oregano. The other shacks hold larger tools and hay, while a windowless structure houses Zaharoula (Little Sugar), an eight-year-old gray-white mare. In front of all these structures, the father has built a sink, comprising a spigot at the end of a water pipe that juts out of the ground, a concrete basin, and a small thatched roof to shield the user from the sun. Just beyond the sink, three posts support one end of a long wooden bar. A forked branch of a nearby olive tree supports the other end, so that the bar is suspended some seven feet above the ground. Here the earth has been cleared of weeds, making it easy to see the hundreds of flies feasting on a dark brown stain.

For Michalis, a city-dweller for nearly half of his thirty-four years, returning here means taking care of his horse. After months of being away, he reacquaints himself with Zaharoula by grooming her. Then it's time for the mare to refresh her trotting and galloping skills. In a nearby field, Michalis holds Zaharoula at the end of a long rope with one hand. In the other, he holds a whip made of a long stick with an elastic rope tied at the end. The horse trots and gallops around him in a large circle. Michalis commands her by calling out "trot" and "gallop" with a Greek accent and occasionally cracking the whip. When the exercise is over, we bring her back to the olive grove, and I help him wash her legs. He tells me that one day he hopes to return here and live and care for Zaharoula more regularly. I don't ask him how he would make a living here, or what his daughters would think of leaving the city, or why he left in the first place. There is no point in any of that. People all over this country are always leaving places such as Agria, and they always long to return.

By dinnertime, we are sitting around a table outside with Michalis's elderly parents and some other relatives who live in Agria year-round. Everyone here is fasting for the forty days before Easter, so dinner is without meat, eggs, or dairy products. Instead, we eat boiled broad beans that his mother has grown in her garden. None of the visitors has observed the fasting rules of Lent, but we say nothing about it. We eat the beans and dip our bread in their oily water. I get some pleasure out of thinking that I am having an authentically simple and traditional experience, but by the end of the meal I am hardly full. Perhaps because everyone is still hungry, talk around the table is of the preparations for Easter. The men plan the roasting of the lamb and the women decide on the side dishes. But for me, a vegetarian, the planned feast offers little solace. The menu on Sunday will feature roasted lamb, roasted lamb innards, and some mayonnaise-drenched version of potato salad. With the sun setting, I try to forget about the hunger in store for me and get ready for church. Tonight the congregation will commemorate Christ's death with a symbolic funereal procession through town.

> Fasting means looking at but not tasting any of the goodies spread out on the kitchen table. Not until Sunday can we eat the cookies, the cakes, or the red-dyed eggs. I am fasting so that I can receive communion. My mother is making me fast. I am hungry. My mother is napping. I am hungry. My mother will not find the egg shells if I wrap them in a napkin and hide them under my bed. I'm still hungry.

At nightfall, a crowd of some two thousand people gathers in the street outside the church, each of us holding an unlit candle. The church building can accommodate only a fraction of the churchgoers, so most of us are waiting in the street for the procession to begin. The out-of-towners have returned to Agria, and now the village feels much bigger than it is. Candlelight from a single candle inside the church spreads from person to person. And in the act of sharing that light, people, who have not seen each other since last Easter, exchange greetings in hushed tones. Michalis, perhaps because he is a professional athlete, seems especially popular among the older folks, who ask him about life in Athens, about his team, and about his family. He tells them that he is playing for a new team, and that he now has a third daughter. Another year has passed. In a moment, the exchange is over. Another year will pass. They might see each other again soon, but, most likely, not until next Good Friday.

On Saturday morning, we return to the olive grove. A father and his young son have also driven here in a pickup truck, from which they have unloaded a lamb no bigger than a skinny, medium-sized dog. Michalis's father, a strong and stout man in his seventies, takes the animal by the rope around its neck and ties it to a post. Bleating, the lamb runs the length of the rope until its neck jerks back, and then tries again. And again. I hear Michalis's father say that the lamb's owner can return in three hours. Michalis and I, too, leave for another exercise session with Zaharoula. This time, he mounts her and rides around a field. By the time we return, the lamb is hanging upside down from the wooden bar with its throat slit, its blood staining the ground. I watch Michalis's father and an uncle approach the carcass and go to work. The father cuts off the lamb's front legs with a knife and hands them, one at a time, to the uncle, who places them in a plastic shopping bag hanging from a nearby tree. I don't get to watch much else because Michalis and I are off to run errands. My last image of the lamb is from afar, with part of its intestine hanging from in between its rear legs. (Later, I will learn that sheep are easier to skin than goats, and that the process can take anywhere from fifteen minutes to more than an hour, depending on how difficult it is to pull the skin off.) That night, our own lamb carcass, wrapped in a towel, will rest on the dining-room table. I will ask the uncle how many animals they slaughtered that day. "Not many," he will say. "About ten."

We, the Athenian visitors, spend the rest of Saturday reestablishing the distance between ourselves and the land by becoming tourists. We drive through the villages of Mount Pelion, looking at the houses with their distinctive architectural style and the Aegean spreading out in the distance. Still, it is difficult to leave Athens behind. The narrow village streets are crowded with the cars of visitors who, like us, are seeking a break from life in the city. At the village of Milies, we stop at a monument erected in honor of a group of men executed by the Nazis. Two of the dead are Michalis's relatives. Another would have also made the list had he not, at the last minute, jumped into the nearby gorge and escaped. Michalis's mother later tells me that her family was forced to abandon that village because the Germans razed it. The only people who got to stay, she says, were the Nazi collaborators.

At midnight on Saturday, the moment for which we have all ostensibly waited for forty days proves as fleeting as any other. A priest comes to the entrance of the church and announces to the crowd amassed outside that Christ is resurrected. "Christ has risen," we say over the din of firecrackers and church bells. "He has truly risen." We hold lit candles; we embrace. Here is Easter, here is the one true God, the promise of eternal life, the family reunited, the village revisited. I don't think anyone knows what to do with all of this, so people just cup their hands around their candle flames and head home. If there is an awkward space that follows, tradition soon crowds it out. Like us, most sit down for a meal of *magiritsa*, a soup of lamb liver and small intestine, which is intended to ease one back into eating after the long fast. Wishing to avoid any fuss, I say nothing about my vegetarian ways, and I bring a few spoonfuls to my mouth. As we eat, I think that this evening would not have gone any differently in either Athens or New York. I go to bed wondering whether, for the Athenians who made the trip here, the place makes Easter feel different, more spiritual.

In the morning, I wake up to the preparations of the great feast. By 8 a.m., the lamb has been skewered, partially wrapped in wax paper, and laid across its back on the patio table. Here is no lamb chop neatly packed in a white Styrofoam tray under fluorescent light, or some rack of lamb adorned with sprigs of rosemary at a fancy restaurant. Here is what you get when you take a young sheep, slit its throat, peel its skin back, cut off its front legs, rip out its guts, and push a long metal rod through its rectum and out its skull. What is left is not only a piece of meat but a record of dying. Death is most pronounced in the traces of life that the butcher's knife has left behind—the bulging eyeballs on each side of the conical head, the open mouth with its rows of white teeth, the hind legs. This animal was bred to be eaten. In that formula, death is only a necessary step, which merits neither any thought nor any disguise.

Now Yiannis, one of the sons-in-law, comes over with wire and pliers in hand to secure the lamb onto the skewer. It's important to bind the neck and legs so that they do not dangle during the roasting, as well as to fasten the chest cavity so that our meal does not slip off the skewer. Yiannis's hands work the wire like those of a seasoned electrician. When he is finished, he and another man lift the animal by the ends of the long metal rod and set it over a long trough of smoldering coals. The roasting takes place in the street, and Michalis is the first of the men who take turns sitting on a plastic lawn chair and rotating the skewer. With the lamb in place, the women go to work on the animal's major internal organs. The lungs, the liver, the heart, and other parts I have trouble identifying, which have been sitting in a large plastic bowl, are now cut in large cubes and passed through a narrow skewer about eight feet long. When the skewer is full, Michalis's sister, Marianthi, turns the long rod so that its pointed end fits into the groove of a small marble slab that is placed on the floor. Another woman, Maria, then stands on a chair to reach the top of the skewer and begins rotating the rod in its groove. The rotation allows Marianthi to wrap the animal's small intestine around the organ chunks, securing them in place for roasting. The end result is something that looks like a long, chunky sausage, what in Greek is called *kokoretsi*. This skewer, too, goes over its own smaller trough of coals, leaving only a bloody windpipe on the patio table. Over the next four hours, the division of labor has the men staring at the roasting lamb and *kokoretsi*, and the women relegated to the courtyard, occasionally serving snacks to the men. The talk around the barbecue is of the lamb's progress, the need to shuffle the coals, the speed at which the skewer ought to be turned. All of it is accompanied by *tsipouro*, a potent alcoholic drink made from the bagasse of grapes. Much of the fun, I begin to understand, is in the talking about the roasting of the lamb, in the anticipation of eating it.

The lamb is ready when the bone joints come apart at the shoulders and the hips. It is then broken off in large chunks and brought to the patio table in heaping stainless-steel platters, which are emptied almost as soon as they arrive. There are some twenty of us gathered around the long table and only a single lamb. I eat none of the meat, filling up instead on bread, salad, and hard-boiled eggs, but no one notices in the excitement. A radio blares out folk music and the sun feels hot on my head. I have drunk too much; we all have, so that we move things around the table a little carelessly, eat a little sloppily. Soon the long table is awash in greasy bones, mustard stains, eggshells, warm beer, and soda cans. When the feeding frenzy slows down, Michalis's mother gets up to dance. Father and son join her, and for a moment the family, which was separated when the son left for Athens, is reunited. The three of them seem to forget about the rest of us and lose themselves in the dignified steps of the *tsamiko*, a folk dance. And I understand that everything—the planning, the trip, the lamb—has been the buildup to this: father, mother, and son just dancing. The moment is short-lived. And I sense that the dancers and those who are watching them know it. This is not how things are. Michalis lives in Athens; the parents are aging; the music is of another time; it is Easter.

But even if all the eating and drinking made us forget somehow that we were only visitors in this place, some insidious fleas soon have us headed back to Athens. Every morning since we have been here, the children have awakened with clusters of red bumps on their bodies, more each day. We weren't sure what was causing them until we began to spot the springy little pests on our own bodies and in our own beds. Each new bite on her children has made my cousin more and more upset. Sensing her daughter-in-law's patience diminishing, Michalis's mother has responded by blaming the infestation on an orphaned and sickly kitten, which has recently moved into the house. Now it seems that every time my cousin or her children complain about the bites, the mother-in-law takes the kitten in her lap and soaks her in antiflea spray. At the end of each such session, the mangy little thing staggers off, seeming even closer to death than before. But while the spraying may be killing the kitten, it is doing nothing to curtail the onslaught of fleas. They have laid their eggs in our rooms, ensuring that their progeny will continue the work that they started. By Monday morning, the day after Easter, my cousin's patience has run out, and the family decides to head back to Athens.

The atmosphere in the car is tense and heavy. Mother and children in the backseat are silent, half-sleeping. Michalis does not take his eyes off the road. After a long time, I break the silence by asking him how he feels. He tells me that, being an athlete, he is used to disappointment. I try to cheer him by telling him that I think we all had a good time. "We did," he says. "It's just that I wanted to come here and do my thing." We fall silent again, and I pass the time counting the quarries alongside the hot and dry highway. As we enter the city, the children wake up, and it is only then that the mood in the car begins to lift. A pop song comes over the radio and Katerina, the middle child, who is four, sings along. In the late afternoon, Athens still feels deserted. As we pull into our parking space, we remark on how well we beat the traffic.

8   ON FOOT

Late one afternoon, I am headed home through the narrow, now quiet streets of Plaka, the city's old town. I keep my bearings by glancing up at the Acropolis every once in a while, the ancient hill rising in the middle of this section of Athens. Like everybody else, I walk in the street because the sidewalks are nonexistent, too narrow, or blocked by parked cars and motorbikes. At the sound of approaching traffic, I will move to the side. But when two dark, shiny sedans approach from my left at the intersection, there is no need to move. The cars glide across a left turn, cutting ahead of me. The car in front is black, sports a Greek flag, and has no license plates. The second car is smaller, blue, and has a matching siren stuck on the roof above the driver's seat.

I am reminded that Athens can be a small place, where at any moment one can spot a dignitary, a celebrity, or a neighbor. But that cerebral reaction is immediately replaced by a more visceral one. Up ahead, the sedans have stopped, and armed guards in blue uniforms and men in dark suits are standing around. In their midst stands the country's stout Archbishop Christodoulos Paraskevaides, having his hand kissed and his robes straightened. I am excited, as if seeing him in person endows me with the power to break through the barrier of television, where my relationship with this high priest has been confined. But just as I am about to be impressed with myself, I hear a woman telling a friend, "All of them we pay for."

I think to myself that this is the perfect Greek moment, where notions of official prestige, institutional power, and high-minded democratic ideals fizzle. Neither the archbishop's guards, nor his carefully cultivated image can shield him from my fellow passerby's acid tongue. Not that the archbishop isn't powerful. This is a man who heads an institution that predates the nation by centuries, and whose blend of religious fundamentalism and nationalism once nearly toppled the government. (The archbishop organized huge protests in 2000 when the government announced plans to drop religious affiliation from new state-issued identity cards. The next year, Greece's Council of State ruled that the inclusion of religion on the cards is unconstitutional.) But power and stature here seem to inspire their own undoing. Instead of energizing the sort of fantasy that makes it easier for rulers to rule—illusions of statesmanship, wisdom, and sanctity—power and stature provoke criticism and highlight the difference between ordinary life and the privileges of the political elite.

The vigilance and skepticism with which Greeks view their public figures, however, are not accounted for solely by this difference. There is something else, something more ambiguous, at work here. Perhaps there hasn't been enough time in Greece for some fantasy of political stature and benevolent leadership to be believed. The Greek state was officially founded in 1827, and the Municipality of the Athenians, as it is called, came into existence only in 1835. The only institution with any significant longevity has been the Greek Orthodox Church. But even the Church, as a centralized, awe-inspiring institution, has been largely invisible from daily life. Instead, there has been ritual, the local church, and the priest, who sits drinking coffee in the square with the rest of his parishioners. Or perhaps there has been too much time, too much history. Political instability, corruption, scandal, war, and foreign intervention have been the stuff of the last two hundred years. In the span since this nation was founded, its leaders have turned on each other and on the people; they have sided with tyrants, killers, and other assorted monsters, while, all along, they have stolen from the public coffers and cheated on their wives. The political stability and democracy that Greece now enjoys have only been a phenomenon of the last quarter-century, and they have come at the price of having a single, but increasingly corrupt party in power for most of those years.

The people, of course, perhaps exhausted by the precariousness of their politics, seem willing to fool themselves some of the time. In the 1990s, the deaths of several prominent public figures transformed them into demigods. The funerals of Prime Minister Andreas Papandreou, the actress and activist Melina Mercouri, and the actress Aliki Vougiouklaki took on mythic dimensions. People mourned en masse, made speeches, paraded the coffins through the streets of Athens, and subsequently named streets and children in their memory. These public figures had marked life here for decades. And their deaths, I suspect, confirmed in people's minds that Greece, as they knew it, was finished. But even in these public funerals, where so many people were willing to believe myths of greatness, there was an informality that worked against the mythification of the dead. People attending the funerals looked hot and uncomfortable on television. Mobs of people joined the processions of the coffins to the cemetery, and people jostled each other for a good spot around the tombs. Even the gunsalute ceremonies looked and sounded haphazard.

On a visit to see a friend who works in the parliament building, formerly a palace, this informality is amplified. I have permission to enter from the back, and I make my way to a reception area the size of a tennis court. An expensive-looking, well-worn red carpet covers the floor. The walls are wood paneled and bare, adorned only by an 8-by-10 framed photograph of Mr. Papandreou. The photograph looks too small for these tall walls, and its placement is somewhat precarious. Hanging from a nail, the image of the late prime minister attests to his deified status within his Panhellenic Socialist Movement, but also suggests that, even after so many years in power, the socialists feel as if they may need to pack up in a hurry one of these days. For the moment, however, everyone here is moving at a leisurely pace. Women sit behind desks, lined up side by side, along two adjoining sides of the room. Floor fans circulate cigarette smoke together with the hot afternoon air coming in from the open windows. One woman, who is older and who, unlike the others, looks professional, seems to be working around her colleagues. The rest are talking so loudly and freely that I feel a bit embarrassed. The current prime minister is, I learn, working just behind the closed office door to my left. I wonder if the noise bothers him. While I don't know the man, later I imagine that it doesn't, that he doesn't even notice. I imagine that at the end of the workday he packs his briefcase and strolls right through this room. A few guards fall in around him, and, in accord with his neosocialist persona, he walks the handful of blocks to his apartment in the posh Kolonaki district.

On his way, he may pass some of his ministers or some of his most bitter political rivals, taking their lunch in Kolonaki Square, alongside young men doing their best to emulate Wall Street yuppies, and older, well-tanned women, shopping for their next Louis Vuitton accessory. The prime minister will walk by, perhaps exchanging a pleasantry with one of the café patrons. The men, who rarely look at each other as they speak, but whose eyes dart here and there to see who is coming and going, will discreetly point out the country's leader. Then the men may stop speaking into their mobile phones for a moment, just as they do each time a woman in tight pants walks by. The prime minister will then feel his leg muscles straining as he ascends the final stretch of this hill leading to his apartment. And as he sits down for his own lunch, still able to hear the din of the square, someone will turn on the television so that the prime minister may watch himself and the other news-makers he has just passed in the square.

There is little in Greek politics that approaches the sense of awe with which the Americans view their presidents, or the British their royals. In turn, the ruling elite do little to inflate their own stature. As a result, the relationship between the state and the people becomes direct, informal, irreverent. Now my encounter with the archbishop comes to mind again, and I tell myself that if vestiges of ancient Athenian democracy sur-vive, they are to be found on the narrow streets of this city. It is in their irreverence that Greeks retain a sense of liberty. But the more time I spend here, the more I also sense that out of this informality, this sacrilegiousness, something crude, reck-less, and corrupt also comes through.

The lack of established institutions engenders a disregard for the law and reinforces, it seems to me, the notion of every man for himself. Everything is there to be used, appropriated, consumed, depleted, and discarded. The faster one moves, the more one is able to outsmart those around one, the more auda-cious and aggressive, the better. That this way of living creates a palpable neglect for others and makes life seem corrupt is either of no consequence, or something to leave behind every time there is a three-day weekend. I try to sort out these thoughts on a walk along the Athenian southern coast, from the sections of Voula to Glyfada. In Greece, a country with an endless coastline and countless islands, the law says that there is supposed to be regular public access to the country's water-front. But everywhere along my walk, cafés and restaurants are perched right on the water's edge. At one point I run across an amusement park that has been set up here—the Ferris wheel giving its riders expansive views of the Saronic Gulf, but sparing no glimpse from the coastal road where I am standing. From the many patrons at these waterfront establishments, I gather that few mind the blocked access. These buildings were likely grandfathered in when the law was passed, or, as is often the case, they are simply overlooked by government inspectors. A similar disregard for law enforcement becomes apparent to me with every step along my route. At the marinas I pass, signs forbid cars from driving onto the piers and parking near the water. But everywhere there are parked cars. In Glyfada's central square, crossing the street is a death-defying experience. On a Saturday afternoon in May, both the roads and the sidewalks are packed with motorists. Street corners often lack traffic lights; cars approach from every direction simultaneously, and pedestrians must dodge cars in order to cross. A friend jokes that in the city, pedestrians do not have the right of way; they have cars. But really what people have are varying amounts of money, with which to either drive across the intersection or not, to have a yacht at the marina or not, to take up a piece of the waterfront or not.

Money, however, only adds choices, for there is always something to take here and someone to take it. Those for whom the waterfront in Glyfada is too expensive need simply move northwest along the coast. There are cheap sea views to be had in a place like Perama, where apartment buildings look as if they were struggling to hold onto the hillside above the container port. An uncle of mine remembers working construction at night in Perama some fifty years ago. The hillside was still bare then, the land there for the taking, if one had money to bribe the local cop and hire a construction crew adept at building quickly in the dark. People would claim land, this uncle tells me, by choosing a spot on the hill and then throwing a stone. Where the stone landed marked the edge of one's new seaside estate. Now those shacks my uncle helped build, legalized long ago, are giving way to apartment buildings of various shapes and sizes—all ugly, all with balconies from which to take in the view of Shell and BP oil storage tanks, the air heavy with diesel fumes.

Those for whom the seaside is not a requirement and land grabbing is not an option can head inland to Gerakas. The expansion of the city in this northeasterly direction is officially sanctioned, rendering moot any concerns about proper land use, efficient transportation, or environmental protection. And while the new Gerakas would fail on all three counts, here the city is applying some of the lessons it has learned after decades of unplanned development. The apartment buildings are only two or three stories high, encircled by small gardens. Terracotta tiles on every roof make them seem like large homes instead of apartment buildings and they preclude any awkward additions from being built later. But even in this brand of new development, earlier lessons are overlooked: Sidewalks are nonexistent or too narrow, because people have built to the edge of their properties; the width of the roads is determined by the size of the private properties on either side, not by urban planners; and the construction of a central sewage system lags behind the issuance of building permits. Still, this plain is filling with rows of new homes.

In Gazi, a neighborhood named after the city's old gasworks, there is neither a sea view to vie for nor any promise of suburban bliss. And, until recently, any taking was confined to the poor—Greeks, Gypsies, and immigrants—seeking an affordable place to live among the crumbling homes. Now, however, the poor are competing for space with the rich, who suddenly have discovered value in the traditional signs of poverty: urban decay, proximity to industrial plants, and cheap real estate. Investors are opening up fancy restaurants that satisfy an appetite for heightening one's eating experience by surrounding oneself with traces of the working class. For the price of dinner in such a setting, one gains entry to some fantasy of what it is like to be poor, which I imagine excites the diner by bringing into focus his ability to traverse class boundaries or by anchoring his life, experienced largely through consumption, in the stuff of manual labor and physical survival. Gazi is a neighborhood where the stucco is falling away from the exterior walls of homes to reveal not bricks but variously sized stones, telling of a time when the local factory workers did not plan the building of these structures, but improvised it. But the expensively renovated buildings, which now house bars and restaurants, give the sense of a wealthier past, while structures too dilapidated to renovate are being demolished, nullifying the past altogether.

The gentrification of Gazi has its roots in the publicly funded conversion of the old gasworks into a cultural complex, which includes a municipal radio station, a theater, and an exhibition hall. In a pamphlet about the conversion, I read that the project, dubbed *Technopolis*, represents an exemplary way to reuse industrial sites in our postindustrial age. With its renovated smokestacks and newly built cobblestone pathways, Technopolis speaks of the progress that Athens has made. The idle smokestacks signal that the city has achieved the means to rid itself of a plant where men and women toiled long hours and to replace it with a space where people come during their leisure time. I, myself, have come to see an exhibit of ancient Greek technology. After some time wandering among sundials, odometers, cranes, and public works contracts on stone tablets, I decide to take a walk around the complex. I snap photographs of the old factory, trying to capture the transformation of the place. But when I turn my camera on a pile of garbage outside the exhibition hall, a member of the grounds crew rushes over to tell me that photography is forbidden. Do I have permission to photograph? I shouldn't be photographing without permission. I didn't know, I say. I have taken only a couple of shots. He wants to know if they are for "personal use." They are. "I hope they don't show up in some magazine," he says, "and send us running." The progress inherent in the conversion of a polluting factory to a cultural center is apparently too fragile to photograph, so I put my camera away and watch the stray dogs meandering around the grounds.

Weeks later I stumble upon a place where the informality and irreverence with which people deal with the structures of power here seem indistinguishable from the crudeness and corruption I see all around me. I walk onto the tiny campus of Pantios University, where students are ostensibly preparing themselves to take their own places in this city. In the meantime, having little to take, they seem to be taking from themselves. Student elections are under way, and the campus, which is now deserted, looks as if a tornado had touched down on it. The country's political parties dominate student politics, which means that students reenact the same sort of factionalism that grips the rest of the country each time there are general elections. On this campus, the length of a city block, the zest of political conviction and devotion to these parties is expressed in signs and posters that are pasted on the walls of the university, the windows, the ground, everywhere. Torn banners hang overhead, and beer cans and flyers are everywhere underfoot. For a moment, I feel as if I am walking through the detritus of a rowdy party, whose carnivalesque energy I can still feel in the air. But among the beer cans, there are signs that read, VICTORY TO INTIFADA and STUDENTS AGAINST WAR AND CAPITALISM. The Greek Communist Party has supplied its young supporters with posters that show a boy hurtling a stone and that read, DOWN WITH THE NEW ORDER OF THE IMPERIALISTS. SOLIDARITY WITH THE PEOPLE OF PALESTINE. There are countless other slogans painted on walls and plastered on the sidewalks. In the exuberance of political expression, I sense both a liberating force and a destructive rage. I think of the stultifying conservatism and political apathy that marked my fellow students at Cornell University during the 1980s and feel envious about the extent of political activity here. But the mess and the vandalism of the grounds also remind me that Greek students often turn on their own universities, destroying classrooms and setting fires as forms of political protest. In a university system with few resources, the students end up damaging the very place that bestows their student status; they hurt themselves in the name of some political party.

In Athens, there is always something to take and someone to take it. There is no need to walk along the coast, or to travel to Perama, Gerakas, or Gazi to see it. The surrounding mountains, visible from any rooftop, tell the story. Where the mountainsides have not been developed, they are bare, but development and bareness are two sides of the same coin—both symptoms of people making a life for themselves at any cost to the land, to their neighbors, to the future. The unchecked development is simply the more modern outcome of a chronic recklessness: irresponsible land use, overcrowding, and policies that sought to convert the economy from agriculture to industry by moving people from the countryside to the city. The bareness of the mountains speaks of soil erosion brought about by the overgrazing of another era, and the ever-popular practice of setting fire to public land. The legacy of the mountains is apparent in every direction. In the south, the Saronic Gulf is still struggling to recover from decades of serving as the city's cesspool. And up above, the city is haunted by what people here call *nefos*, a dark cloud of poisonous smog that comes and goes according to temperature and wind direction, but that is always fed by the Athenians' great love for their cars.

9 GRANDFATHER

Grandfather, a shrunken eighty-seven-year-old man, with cool blue eyes and thick, snow-white hair, lies crookedly across his hospital bed. If you knew him when he was younger, you would be able to see traces of his lady-killer good looks behind the bandages and the nose tube that's draining his stomach of a thick, brown juice. In his long, proud face I find all the makings of his charming, playful smile, but there is nothing now to set them in motion.

For two days, Grandfather has complained of excruciating abdominal pain as we—seven of his children and grandchildren—have watched his gut balloon. The doctors think that some part of his intestines has twisted into a knot. Unless they operate, the intestines may burst and Grandfather will die. That diagnosis was made in the early afternoon. When I arrive at the hospital, it is past nine in the evening, and he is still waiting to be called to the operating room. The doctors never explain why they postpone the operation every couple of hours, but it's easy to guess. With only one operating room in service, younger people have priority.

As a retired hotel waiter, Grandfather relies on the Greek public health system. On paper, Greece promises its working people free, high-quality health care at a nationwide network of hospitals and outpatient clinics. In reality, the system is rotten. The extent and quality of care depend on an institutionalized practice of bribery, a stomach for putting up with inattentive doctors and clinicians who enjoy civil service protections, and a good deal of luck.

The sight of the hospital building to which Grandfather has been admitted only heightens my sense of what he is up against. The tall, old-fashioned windows that have been pushed open on this warm spring evening make the building look disheveled and chaotic, and the lack of air-conditioning hints at a wider technological inadequacy. A sign on the front door says that visiting hours are between 4 and 8 in the evening, but no one stopped me when I walked in at 9 p.m. (When I decide to get some air later that night, I will find the same door bolted from the inside. But I will simply slide the bolt back and walk out, leaving the door unlocked.) Inside, the place is poorly lit and dirty. The high ceilings and the panes of frosted glass above each door make me feel as if I have walked back in time. There is no public elevator, only a set of well-worn marble steps.

Grandfather's room was made to accommodate two beds, but a third one has been squeezed in. All three beds are occupied. At the far end of the room, there is an elderly woman, who lies motionless near the window; on the bed against the right wall, a man with a cloudy eye holds a full urine bag; Grandfather's bed is on the left, near the door. People visiting the woman occupy one of the two metal chairs in the room, and Grandfather's family control the other. There are no partitions, no curtains to be drawn around each patient. A single light switch controls a row of harsh fluorescent lights.

We walk in and out of the room, not speaking very much, trying to reassure each other that Grandfather will be all right. He opens his eyes only once in a while, when he detects something unusual in the commotion around him. His eyes lock onto mine when he hears my voice for the first time. There is disdain and bitterness in his gaze, as if he is ashamed for me to find him in this condition. I try to cheer him up with a smile, but he just closes his eyes. Soon orderlies come to take him to the operating room. As he is wheeled away, we offer him words of encouragement. My relatives have chosen not to tell him that he is going to have surgery, and now he is too sedated to ask.

On Christmas Eve, I sit between my grandfather and my father on my parents' bed and watch TV. We are wearing our pajamas, eating dried chickpeas and raisins, and sipping our drinks. They, because they are adults, drink brandy, which is too strong for me. But I can have vermouth.

The operating room is one floor below his room. Three chairs next to the marble staircase make up the waiting area. When we arrive, two of the three chairs are occupied by men who are smoking. A few feet away a large red sign announces that smoking is forbidden. It is not their cigarette smoke that bothers me, but their gall. I feel myself getting angry, although I know in the back of my mind that my anger over the conditions in the hospital and the delay in treating my grandfather has been building ever since I entered this place. I walk over, calmly inform them of the no smoking policy, and ask them to put out their cigarettes. One complies; the other says he will put it out but keeps on smoking. I stand over him wishing he would provoke me, but he simply moves to an open window. I feel like tossing him out of it, but I don't. None of the hospital staff is around to enforce the smoking ban.

We wait around wondering what's happening, taking turns sitting in the chairs, and chewing on cookies and chocolate bars. None of us has eaten anything else for hours, and there is no place in the hospital serving meals. Our only news comes from an orderly who tells us that more than an hour after he entered the operating room, Grandfather is still waiting for his operation. As we wait, I learn from my uncle that he had to fight to have Grandfather admitted in the afternoon. The hospital administrators had said that there were no available beds, and they had suggested that Grandfather try another hospital. As Greeks will do in such situations, my uncle walked around the hospital looking for a doctor he knew worked there, whom he would ask to intervene. It was then that this uncle accidentally walked into a room with three empty beds; he then tried another, and another, finding numerous empty beds. Still, the administrators refused admission. They relented only when my uncle bribed them. In the hours that followed, we figured out that the empty beds in this hospital, and most likely in many other public hospitals, are controlled by the affiliated doctors. In cahoots with these doctors, the administrators will refuse admission to patients who just walk in, safeguarding a system where doctors dole out hospital admissions to their own patients in exchange for bribes. Those who either lack a connection to such a doctor or do not have the money are simply turned away.

> For the first time in my life, I have not slept at all in the night because of an earache. It is still dark out when my mother rouses me from bed and helps me get ready. I know it is important to get to the clinic as early as we can so that we can get a number. When we do, my mother and I glance at the white slip of paper and feel relieved. I think it is the first time we have gotten a number under ten, which means that we will not have to spend the entire day waiting in the hallway to see a doctor.

It's past 11 p.m. when Grandfather's own internist arrives and promises to take care of things. He vanishes behind the doors of the operating room. The next time we see him, it's about an hour later when he summons my uncle, Grandfather's son and the leader of our contingent. The operation has been a success. The intestines were not twisted. Instead, there was a tear near the top of the small intestine. If the doctors had waited a little while longer, Grandfather would have been poisoned as half-digested food and digestive juices leaked into his system. Now could my aunt leave the internist and my uncle alone? While the surgeons are finishing up inside, there is business to be discussed. In the ensuing tête-à-tête, the internist strongly recommends to my uncle that he reward the two surgeons, the resident, and the anesthesiologist with a total of seven hundred euros (about $700). He, himself, of course, has earlier been paid for his supervisory services; he would not be here otherwise. To ensure that my uncle heeds the internist's recommendation, one of the surgeons appears at the door of the operating room, with Grandfather's blood on his white surgical gown. No, the operation is not yet complete. The surgeon is betting that a look at the bloodstains will speed up business. If asked, the surgeon would, of course, say that he had come to reassure the family, but he would be hard pressed to explain why he had not waited to stitch Grandfather up before he came out. The timing makes this charade especially cruel, but apparently necessary in the minds of these doctors, who seem to think that we might refuse to pay if we were not forced to think of Grandfather, with his abdomen cut open, on their operating table.

At 12:30 a.m., the seven of us huddle in the dark hallway outside the operating room to come up with the money. The transaction ends upstairs about an hour later. My uncle is now asked by the two surgeons and the anesthesiologist to enter a small office next to Grandfather's room. The meeting will supposedly give the doctors an opportunity to inform my uncle about Grandfather's condition, but everyone knows the session will simply provide the privacy needed for the payoff. The doctors will apparently see to it that the resident, who is absent from this meeting, gets his cut. While the payment is being made, Grandfather is returned to his bed. The nurse flips on the lights and jars the other patients from their sleep. My aunt has already had to inform the one nurse on duty of Grandfather's imminent return, and she has had to insist that the nurse prepare his bed. Grandfather is moaning and calling for his mother on the stretcher; he screams when he is transferred to his bed. Someone tips the orderly who has just wheeled him from the operating room. Soon we will have to bribe the nurse in order to secure her care for the night. But the forty euros (about $40) she eventually pockets will only buy us part-time service. My aunt, who will spend the night at the hospital, receives instructions from the surgeons for the rest of the time. They tell her that she has to make sure Grandfather does not pull at his various tubes and bandages, and she has to keep an eye on the intravenous feeding tube, to make sure it doesn't bend. Her task seems difficult because Grandfather is extremely agitated. The doctors say that his agitation is a reaction to the anesthesia. To me, he just seems angry at being deceived. At about two in the morning, we wish my aunt strength and we leave.

In this system, money doesn't buy one privileges or better care, just the most basic services—an explanation from the doctors about one's condition, a nurse to change the IV, not much else. Refusing to pay is to risk death at worst, or serious neglect at best. Perhaps it is the low salaries of doctors who participate in the public health care system that fuel this system of illicit payments, or perhaps it is the ease with which doctors can make small fortunes that sustains the extortion. The corruption is so ingrained in the system that the people who experience it take the payoffs for granted. Most have no choice. Bribing public doctors is more affordable than private health insurance and private hospitals. It also seems difficult to complain about the corruption when one is trying to get well. I see this eagerness to put our troubles behind us when Grandfather is released from the hospital. No one is in the mood to talk about the last ten days. Everyone just seems glad that Grandfather is recovering and that we got him out of that hospital alive.

I spend the months that follow in New York and Grandfather spends them in and out of the city's public hospitals as his health deteriorates. The next time I see him, it's in a coffin. Having landed in Athens on a crisp, bright November morning, I have just enough time to change clothes and make it to the funeral. Grandfather died the day before on some hospital bed with his daughter and my cousins around him. His body was then turned over to a funeral home, which has arranged his burial for today. There are no lengthy wakes in Greece. My relatives last saw Grandfather at the hospital, and they will see him one last time shortly.

The municipal cemetery is built on the side of Ymittos, a mountain that flanks the city to the east. Because no burials are performed at this public facility on the weekend, everyone who died in the area over the last two days is being buried on Monday. All around us are groups of mourners in various stages of their own funeral services. People stand around a grieving woman, who cries quietly and looks near collapse; another group lines up behind the pallbearers, who must lean forward to make it up the steep mountainside; there are also those who mill around, smoking and talking during some odd moment in all that goes on here. Past the cemetery gates, there is a new church that is being built on the right, and an older chapel full of people to the left. Everywhere else, there are tombs with pine and cypress trees growing among them. Our funeral director leads us up a gravel path to a low white rectangular structure, just past the gate. The building has four identical, evenly spaced glass doors on one of its long sides. Wreaths of white flowers, with ribbons showing the names of the dead in gold lettering, have been propped up against the wall between the doors. The funeral director tells us that our entrance is the one on the far right.

The door opens onto a small room, with gray marble floors and a stand for a coffin. There are three other identical rooms here, only partially separated from each other. The dividing walls extend to within a few feet of the building's façade, so that standing by the front door I can see across the length of this structure and into the adjacent room. We wait around for Grandfather to be carried in, the silence in our section interrupted only by the cries of the mourners next to us, who have just gotten their first glimpse of their dead. Their shock, a portent of what we are about to go through, makes it difficult for me to stand still. When the people next to us grow quieter, we hear the cries of other mourners farther down the hall. When I don't think I can stand it anymore, Grandfather's coffin is brought in through a side door. "Do you want the casket open or closed?" asks one of the cemetery workers. "Open, open," calls out a woman, who I later learn was Grandfather's caregiver. "There's nothing to hide." She has invited herself to the funeral. "We have to ask," says the worker apologetically.

When the workers pull the lid off, only Grandfather's face is visible. A mound of white flowers, which create a look so over-the-top, so artificial that it only heightens the reality of his death, covers the rest of him. It is our turn to cry. Grandfather's daughter caresses his face and calls out for her daddy. The caregiver, too, makes a lot of noise, but she's just being histrionic. Distant relatives I have never seen before take turns leaning over and kissing him on the forehead. I think of all the years together he and I missed and I hold myself up against a corner of the room.

After about ten minutes, I step outside to get some fresh air, but realizing that, in a short while, I will never see Grandfather again, I go back in. In all, we spend no more than thirty minutes around the coffin. When our time is up, a group of pallbearers in worn tuxedos enter the room and inform us that it is now time to move to the chapel. We mill outside the building for a moment, as they square the coffin on their shoulders. A little farther away, a new group of mourners awaits, preparing to move into the room we have just left.

The pallbearers transport Grandfather to the chapel, where a team of priests and cantors has been at it all morning. The coffin lid again comes off, and we, the closest of his relatives, are asked to file in around him. Speaking quickly, the priests race through the requisite prayers and blessings, and we do our best to keep up. In a way, Grandfather—I mean this man who spent his childhood working as an errand boy in Cairo, who parachuted out of airplanes in World War II, who seduced women, married, divorced, and fathered three children, who brought honeycomb for me to eat, this man who grew old— seems beside the point in all of this. His death is subsumed in some Athenian public manager's vision of efficiency—a funereal process that offers neither solace nor time to grieve. Perhaps no funeral can. Death comes too quickly.

We trail his coffin up the mountainside. Walking along a gravel path and up a concrete-paved road, we reach a cement pit that will be Grandfather's grave. The pallbearers set the closed coffin on the ground, and a priest prays to Christ "to give rest with the Saints to the soul of your servant where there is neither pain, nor grief, nor sighing, but life everlasting." Everything speeds up now. Two cemetery workers move in to pass ropes under the coffin, which they use to lift and lower the box into the pit. Straddling the grave, they strain to balance the weight and keep the thing from sliding off. Someone walks around with a basket of white carnations, exhorting us to take some because "There is no dirt here." I want to slow it all down but I can't. People toss their flowers in the pit; I toss mine too. The workers get hold of a heavy concrete slab and drag it over the grave's opening. They lay the wreaths with the ribbons of Grandfather's name over the slab. And then it's done. There is nothing to do now but walk back.

Our party of mourners drifts down the road, black-clad figures under a bright, cold sun. In the distance between me and them, I grieve for the piece of me that I leave behind on this mountainside. No, Grandfather and I were not close. Our relationship was severed more than twenty years ago when I emigrated to New York. In that time, I grew up and he grew old. I visited him once, ten years ago. He had trouble recognizing me at the airport. Still, for me he was a link to the past, a trace of childhood. "Why did you come?" my relatives have asked me. "Why go into all that trouble?" I want to tell them that I have come to grieve for a lifetime I have spent away from them, for all the years I have lived without Grandfather, for all the time I can never get back. A sob wells up in me, and I give in to it beside the ossuary.

The funeral ends at the cemetery café. It's tradition here that when a person dies, mourners drink sugarless Greek coffee. The ritual used to take place at the grieving family's home, but times have changed. Running a cemetery is a costly public service, and the local municipality is trying to recoup some of the costs by providing a chamber to house the café with enough tables and chairs for a couple of hundred people. The room is nearly empty when we arrive. There is only one other party at the far end and the detritus of mourners who have moved on—white demitasses with muddy bottoms. The few of us who are still here, close relatives and Grandfather's parish priest, sit around a table that has been set with a small bottle of Metaxa brandy and a basket of crunchy biscuits. A waiter brings water, coffee, and small glasses for the brandy. "May his memory be eternal. God forgive him," we say in a joyless toast. The priest talks a little bit about how he had missed Grandfather at church in recent weeks. Someone else remarks about how well planned the funeral was.

That afternoon a few of us gather again, this time at my cousin's home, to act out another funeral tradition: a meal of fish soup. The choice of fish may stem from some faded pagan rite or from Christianity, for which the animals have symbolized the power of faith—as when Christ fed five thousand hungry people with five loaves of bread and two fish—or it may have been a sign of common belief. (The Greek word for fish, *ichthys*, doubles as an acrostic of the initial letters in the

Greek words for Jesus Christ, Son of God, Savior.) But for my aunt, who does the cooking, it's just something that happens after a funeral. She is not interested in the ritual, only in having something to do. I, myself, dislike fish soup, but I eat it anyway.

I stay in Athens long enough to make the requisite memorial nine days after death. With nothing urgently in need of doing, I spend the days wandering around Ano Dafni, a neighborhood where I lived as a boy and where Grandfather spent the last years of his life. In my ramblings, I move about with the certainty and nonchalance of a longtime resident. Only a single sight gives me pause. On my way home one afternoon, I notice my name on a small poster plastered around a telephone pole—a surreal moment during which I can't decide if I am misreading while also trying to figure out what I might have done to deserve such notoriety. In my next step, everything is clear again. The poster, white with a gold border, announces Grandfather's funeral. I bear his name.

On the ninth day after Grandfather's death, we return to the cemetery. This time, it's just my aunt, her two daughters, and me. We carry napkins, a few plastic spoons, and a bowl of *kollyva*: a medley of boiled wheat, raisins, and nuts topped by a layer of sugar. The Eastern Orthodox Church believes that the prayers of the living can help the dead gain God's grace. That is not why we are here. Since his death, there has simply been an unspoken determination to do everything that we are supposed to. For observing custom and ritual, we have been rewarded with the answers about what to do from one moment to the next, but with little else. Today, a Sunday, we are joining tens of others in the cemetery, who have come only to memorialize their dead. Among the graves, people have lit small oil-burning lanterns and laid fresh flowers. Except for a few elaborate graves, most of them are white marble boxes that rise about a foot off the ground. Each has a white marble cross and some include a photograph of the deceased. The faces in the photographs tend to be old, but there are exceptions. No fancy carvings adorn the tombstones and no epitaphs call out to the passersby. Grandfather's grave remains entirely unadorned. In the days since the funeral, the slab over his tomb has been sealed with cement, and the flowers on the wreaths have withered. Under the slab, his body rests in the dirtless concrete pit, ostensibly decomposing with the aid of some chemical that the funeral home added in its preparation for burial. It's not clear to anyone I ask why cemeteries have stopped burying corpses in dirt, but people don't like it. I hear several gruesome stories of bodies exhumed years later from such concrete pits; the bodies had yet to decompose. Lack of cemetery space in Athens necessitates that eventually the dead be dug up and their bones stored in an ossuary.

As I ponder all of this, my relatives look around for a priest who will agree to conduct the memorial service. Finally, they track down an elderly clergyman, who drives around the cemetery in a lime-green, boxy wagon of a car, hoping to offer his services to people just like us. Without much ado, he stands at the foot of the grave, asks for the deceased's first name, and speeds through some religious text reserved for the occasion. He stops his litany only to take the bowl of *kollyva* from my aunt's hands. With his right hand, he makes the sign of the cross over the dish, and then uses a spoon to toss some of the mixture over the grave. *Ean mi o kokkos tou sitou peson . . .*

"Unless the grain of wheat falls into the earth and dies, it remains alone, but if it dies it bears much fruit," said Christ (John 12:24). But I don't think that any of us is dwelling on the symbolism of this moment. This ritual, like all the others that have accompanied this funeral, feels like one more task to be checked off on some to-do list than opportunities for inspiration. When the priest returns the bowl to my aunt, he mouths a few more words and the memorial service is done. One of my cousins hands him a few bills for his services, and he is off to look for his next gig.

As on the day of the funeral, a milky sun makes everything look starkly flat. We have nothing to say as we stand around the grave, except for my aunt, who frets about how to go about ordering a proper monument. Soon, they start down the road. A light breeze moves across the cemetery; the ribbons on the dried wreaths scrape over the slab. "My grandfather, I'll keep you with me." I touch my fingers to the slab. In the distance, I can see my relatives and start in their direction. On the road, a black-clad woman sees me walking by and motions me over. She has a young girl with her, who helps her dish some *kollyva* into a paper cup, which she hands to me. Descending the mountainside, I use a plastic spoon to take mouthfuls of the sweet grain, in memory of someone I never knew.

10 NATIVE ATHENS

A shack used to stand near the end of Agias Lavras Street in the Petroupolis section of Athens. No photographs of it survive, and most people who might have reason to remember it are dead. Anyway, it wasn't memorable, just a hastily built four walls and a tile roof, which was enough to claim the land and to house some family from god knows where. The place had two rooms—one for eating, the other for sleeping—a concrete floor, and a couple of windows. To get to the kitchen and the bathroom, you had to walk out the front door and immediately turn left into a room that was probably added after the shack was built. A garden of weeds, which grew all around, was redeemed only by its trees: a couple of lemon trees in the back, a variety of plum tree whose fruit was small and green, and a tall, unkempt pine tree infested with caterpillars. The fuzzy little worms were everywhere, one behind the other, crawling in long greenish strings. To fight the infestation, sometimes you would have to pour kerosene along the strings and light them. On either side of the shack, there were proper homes with small patios and a few marble steps leading to their front doors. And in the distance, there was the quarry.

The woman who was to become my mother bought the place with her sister in 1965. Their names were on the deed for the property, but it was their brother who sent them the money from America. He had jumped ship in Baltimore, and by that time was in the fifth year of leaving one New York restaurant job for another, hounded by immigration officers. The shack eventually became my mother's dowry, and, in 1970, my first home. Three years later, my parents decided that a shack that let the rain in was no place to raise their son, so we moved. A nun, who rented the shack from us after we left, died there, penniless, a few years later. She was its last resident. We still have one of her Bibles.

I don't know why I have returned here, but I knew that I would. I included all our old neighborhoods—there were four in ten years—on my list of sojourns without thinking, as if it were the most natural thing to do. Perhaps it was because I know these places so well, retracing so often in my mind the streets of my childhood. But I put these neighborhoods at the bottom of the list. There would be a confrontation at each stop, I supposed, some reckoning with the past, with the passing of time, and with all that changed. Part of me, though, has dreaded the moment when, coming around the corner, I would be faced with the old playground, the familiar door, the place that no longer stands. It has not been some plunge into nostalgia that I have been avoiding. I am nostalgic about some things, but this dread is something else.

Petroupolis lies on the city's western edge. The neighborhood stretches to one of the foothills, part of a mountain range that hems the city in to the west, and stops. The area's marginal status made it okay to live in a shack thirty years ago, but no longer. The system in which a landowner allows a developer to put up an apartment building on his or her property in exchange for an apartment in the new structure has transformed the neighborhood. The pharmacy that marks my old bus stop is still in business, but all around it apartment buildings rise where modest single-story homes used to sit. On Agias Lavras Street, tall concrete boxes line both sides of the street, with only a handful of single-family homes remaining and looking out of place. The shack was consumed by the development in 1982, after my parents allowed a developer to raze it and build skyward. In exchange, we got two apartments: a one- and a two-bedroom. We chose to rent them out, but we knew that if we ever needed to live in one, the roof would not leak. What we did not know, never considered, or just dismissed out of hand is that we would be contributing to a wave of unplanned development in Athens, which has created an oppressing combination of building density, congestion, and dangerous effects on the microclimate. For personal gain, we took part in a frenzy of building marked by forgettable architecture, and driven by greed. But who can blame a family of shack owners, or any of the working-class people in Petroupolis who saw a good deal and took it? No one need point a finger. Living in the boxes is hard enough.

> I am small enough that I still sleep in a crib, a tiny bed with wooden railings. It's raining. My mother positions a light blue tub to catch the drops that fall from the ceiling. I fall asleep to the sound of water hitting plastic.

Making my way down the street, I have trouble distinguishing the building that rose on our land from the ones around it. It is only when I spot Mrs. Despina's old house—one of the handful that have not been replaced—that I know the apartment building to the right is where the shack used to be. The building is just twenty years old, but it already looks aged. The concrete is showing signs of wear and the architecture seems dated. Newer apartment buildings are incorporating more curves in their cement molds in what seems like an attempt to embrace some contemporary aesthetic of smoothness. Here, though, every corner makes a right angle, the emphasis having been on stacking the maximum numbers of floors allowed by law and on putting the apartments on sale. The only innovation of sorts is on the ground floor of the five-story structure. The front door opens to a tiny lobby, but most of the ground space is reserved for three or four parking spots—a legal requirement intended to relieve street congestion. From the sidewalk, I can see through to the backyard, where a few trees grow on a small patch of dirt. Among them is a lemon tree, whose survival my mother negotiated with the developer when she gave up the land.

The floor is painted burgundy. Mother rocks her body from left to right as she operates the knitting machine. Behind her, in my playpen, I rock too. She works at home, making sweaters. I keep quiet.

A woman in her fifties stands on the first-floor balcony and stares down at me. She wants to know why I am photographing the house next door. "Have you lived here long?" I counter. "Since 1982," she says. "I lived here," I tell her, "before there was an apartment building. And I was just remembering the old woman who lived next door." She remembers Mrs. Despina too. "You are from that family that lives in America," she says, as I begin to feel more and more awkward about having to explain my return. We cannot find much else to say to each other. What can I tell her about an old shack? What can she tell me about the last twenty years? I head back to the bus stop. It is early afternoon, and children are returning home from school, people are shopping, a construction crew is hard at work. From the bus's rear window, I stare at the neighborhood's main thoroughfare, March 25th Street. Decorative iron railings have been put down to keep cars off the sidewalks, while antique-looking lampposts bring to mind a prosperous past that never occurred here. And in the distance, there is the quarry; the hole in the rock is now an outdoor theater.

More than twenty years of socialist rule and a great deal of European Union money have softened the city's western edge. A quarry has been converted to a public space, schools and youth centers dot the map, and in Bournazi, the neighborhood we moved to after Petroupolis, a drainage canal that doubled as a mosquito incubator is now covered by a new road and lined by saplings struggling to survive the city's heat. Developers have been hard at work here too. New buildings now rise on the dirt lots that once were the children's soccer fields and their hiding places. But for all the public works and private construction, the neighborhood looks and feels like the working-class place I remember. Bournazi is still at the city's margin, looking desolate and dusty in some places, shoddy and improvised in others. The generation of laborers, refugees, and internal immigrants who built the area are still living here. Now, however, additions grow atop their single-story homes for their children and their new families. It's easy to find half-finished construction projects, stalled for lack of money, until the loan goes through. The poor stay poor. No new road, no new apartment building can change that.

Near our old apartment in Bournazi, everything looks the same as it did thirty years ago. The candy store still sells the best pistachio ice cream I have ever tasted, and the bakery is still doing business on the corner, albeit under new ownership. Thirty years ago, the bakery doubled as a communal oven. Housewives too poor to have ovens of their own would bring pans of food here to bake alongside the bread. For a moment, I think I smell food cooking in the bakery's ovens, but the salesgirl behind the counter tells me that no one brings food to bake here anymore. Time has also done away with Stella, the neighborhood's outdoor movie theater, which favored Tarzan movies and anything by the Greek film star Aliki Vougiouklaki. Moviegoers would sit on plastic chairs, chew salted pumpkin seeds, and spit out the shells on the gravel. At intermission, those who could afford it might buy a Coca-Cola and a *kok*, a doughnutlike pastry popular only at the movies. But if you were willing to forgo the amenities and the snacks, and if you did not mind straining to hear the dialogue, then you could just watch the movie at home, as long as your roof was tall enough to peer over Stella's walls.

A couple of blocks from where Stella was, at the end of a nondescript street, stands an old and small house, where we used to live. Like many others in neighborhoods like this one, the house reflects an architectural style abandoned decades ago. A small gate leads into a tiny courtyard. To the right, a door, wrought iron over frosted glass, opens onto the ground floor apartment we once occupied. At the time, the apartment was the only one on this level. Now two more have been squeezed in around the courtyard. A curving staircase on the left leads to one more apartment on the second floor. The courtyard is dark and damp in midday. A small tree is surviving on an even smaller patch of dirt, where I used to bury watermelon seeds. Nothing has come of my work.

> I am not old enough to go to school but steady enough on my feet for Father to teach me how to pass a soccer ball. We stand a few feet apart in the courtyard. Kick it with the inside part of your foot. No, like this. After one or two attempts, I am sure I have mastered passing. Father disagrees. This is the last time I will play soccer with you, he says. He is not lying.

There is no one at home in our old apartment. Perhaps the place has been renovated, but it has not gotten any bigger: a foyer in the center, with the kitchen and the bedroom on either side, a windowless bathroom off the kitchen. For a family with one young child, the apartment was adequate. Nothing leaked, the rent was affordable, and my mother's job was nearby. Now, though, the place looks miserable, even by Athenian standards. Still, the landlord continues to find tenants, for this is western Athens and there are plenty of poor people around.

> Father lands the first blow near the entrance to the bedroom, striking mother sloppily on the cheek. She moves to the kitchen and he follows, his belt in his hand. He is yelling and she's begging him to stop. She dashes into the bathroom and tries to close the door, but he catches it before she can shut it. The door to the bathroom has a pane of frosted glass, through which I can see his blurred figure, flesh-colored, moving.

In Athens, it is not uncommon for people to live near their relatives, in the same house, the same building, or at least in the same neighborhood. I imagine that this proximity among family members helped people cope with the transition from the village to the big city, or from abroad, as in the case of refugees, to the homeland. For my family, where we lived was always dictated by our modest means, but the choice of one working-class neighborhood over another also had to do with where our relatives lived. In 1975, the move from Bournazi and the environs of western Athens to Dafni, closer to the city center, meant we had a bit more money, but also that we were leaving one set of relatives for another. In Petroupolis and Bournazi, we were living near some of my mother's relatives; in Dafni, we were going to be close to my father's family. An aunt and a cousin of mine still live here, and it is they who have kept me coming back over the years.

More than once in that time, I have walked the streets of this neighborhood with the sureness of a local. If the scale of the streetscapes always seems to me so much smaller than I remember, or if I am interested in all the immigrants I see moving about, I don't show it. And now, at an outdoor café in a nearby public square, making mental notes of things as a traveler would, I sip my coffee and glance around like everybody else. In the people who stroll by, I see the neighbors, friends, and lovers I might have had. But I left, and they just walk past me. My only connection is with the square that has changed little in nearly a quarter of a century: the dwarf palms, the bitter orange trees, and boys chasing a soccer ball; the pine trees that still look too big, too lush, as if they are hiding something.

New apartment buildings, painted in pastel yellows and pinks, have sprouted here too. And it is next to them that I notice for the first time how many families still live in the little, single-story houses that people put up in the years after the Second World War. These crumbling homes once housed people, many of whom had abandoned the countryside for the promise of a better life in the capital. Now it is in such places that the city's latest crop of newcomers—immigrants from countries such as Albania, Bulgaria, and Iraq—are trying to make new lives. In the late morning, a hot sun already overhead, the small houses are shuttered and the streets are empty. In the quiet, a cat crosses my path, carrying a kitten by the neck. I stop and stare. The kitten is quite big and every few feet it slips from the cat's oral grip. In Dafni, life eases along. An older woman in black—in mourning—stops and stares with me at the cat and her kitten. They're just like humans in how lovingly they care for their young, she says.

Our old place, the top apartment in a two-story building, is a step up from the little cement cubes. Number 14 on Kresnas Street—the digits written by hand on the white stucco wall—looks exactly the way it did when we left it in 1979. Only the addition of an air-conditioning unit, which was a luxury back then, belies that time has stood still. The bakery around the corner is still here too, but the souvlaki place, whose exhaust vent used to spew smoke from the grilling meat into our apartment, is gone. A plumber has now moved in. In a sign of progress, the small street that was our playground has been closed to car traffic, but our old spots are just as we left them: the white marble steps in front of my friend Thanos's house, the street sign that we pretended was a basketball hoop, the space between the buildings through which I could see my mother calling me to dinner. I spent the best years of my childhood in Dafni, perhaps because it was here that I was first old enough to go to school, make friends, get a sister, and develop a sense of my place in the world. There were also signs that life for our family might be getting better. We bought a stove and a washing machine. I had a new bed, and there was a brown velvet sectional in the living room. We were still poor, but having always been poor I only noticed the changes for the better, not the familiar wants. My mother did piecework at home, gluing boxes or sewing ties, and my father worked in a factory run by the German company AEG. After all this time, the neighborhood seems to be telling the same sort of stories.

> Having returned from work, Father sits down to a meal of fish soup and a concoction of boiled fish chunks topped by homemade mayonnaise and garnished with boiled carrots. I, too, take a seat at the table, even though I'd rather starve than eat this stuff. Mother moves around the kitchen. No one speaks. The next few seconds tick by fast. The plate of fish chunks flies across the room; my mother ducks; the fish sticks to the kitchen door. Years later, the glass on the door remains cracked.

I return to Dafni just as the school day begins at the Fifth Elementary School. At quarter past eight, a whistle blows in the schoolyard, and the children scramble to get in line by grade. Their teachers stand facing them, and a girl is chosen from among the students to lead the entire school in morning prayer. Just as it did twenty-five years ago, the day begins with one Our Father and some 150 children and adults making the sign of the cross. It does not matter that a good number of these students now are not Greek Orthodox—not Christians at all. The children say their prayers while facing a mural of a seascape that adorns the school wall. In the foreground, the mural shows a tropical sandy beach with palm trees on either end. But the tropics quickly give way to more familiar Mediterranean fare: dolphins frolicking in the water and sailboats cruising across the horizon. In the center of the mural, there is a lighthouse, but nowhere are there any people. Beyond the uninhabited paradise, above the wall, a jumble of rooftops, TV antennas, and solar water heaters stretch deep into the haze. But from the schoolyard, the children cannot see the mess.

At the first break, a door opens next to one of the painted palm trees, and the children spread out across the yard. They don't have a sandbox to play in anymore—that's been paved over—but the boys are still using an empty plastic bottle as a soccer ball. Two basketball hoops have been added, a sign of the sport's growing popularity since Greece won the men's European Championship in 1987. The children look like we did, except that we had to wear uniforms—blue, lightweight jackets, which everyone called "aprons." Despite the uniformity, you could still spot the kids from the really poor families. They were always, it seemed to me, a little more unkempt than the rest of us, their "aprons" a bit too short, garlic and sardines on their breath. Now, you can look at children's clothes to tell who is Greek and who isn't. Everyone is in Western children's clothes: Some of the immigrant children's outfits, however, look far from new. But from where I stand, at least, economic and ethnic differences do not seem to matter much. Here are just children playing. An Asian girl, speaking perfect Greek, plays with her friends. And as I walk by, I think that scenes like these may save this country from racism.

I look around the schoolyard for my best friend Elias. The other kids have made up a song to tease us because we are always together. When I find him, I stick my right foot forward and he ties my shoelace. He knows how and I don't.

When the bell summons the children back to class, I wonder what has happened to my classmates, green-eyed Stella, Roula who was my first crush, Nikos, Stratos. Elias is married and now sells plaster lawn ornaments in his father-in-law's store. Another of my classmates, Voula, I'm told, works at her parents' ice-cream shop. For something like a nickel, I could get a taste of every flavor in the store on a wafer cone, and on good days, a dab of whipped cream. Things don't change easily here. Andreas I found years later. We turned up in the same high school in New York. He was going to be a doctor. I don't know about the others. Chances are they are married, raising children, getting by. What's in store for these children here, I wonder. What will they remember of their time in this schoolyard?

> The boys walk home from school, our arms draped
> around each other's shoulders. We talk about the girls and
> our games. When we reach the newspaper kiosk, we set a
> time to meet on the "little block," where we always play.

While the poor stay poor in Athens, the rich seem to multiply in the city, or at least in Nea Penteli, to which we moved on a sad day sometime in the summer of 1979. Nea Penteli was a sparsely built community of villas and sanatoria nestled among pine trees underneath Mount Pentelikon in the northeast outskirts of the city. Today there are more villas than trees here. And a family like ours would be just as out of place now as we were then. Again, however, there was a family connection. Our rich relatives from America, who were also sponsoring our imminent emigration, were building a villa of their own here. We relocated to a small apartment on the ground floor of the construction site to keep an eye on the place and to save on rent before our grand trip. When we arrived I remember knowing two things about the area: that the nearby quarry had been supplying the finest marble anywhere since the time of Phidias, and that a military base, perhaps one with U.S. nuclear weapons, was located on the mountain. Staring at some communications installations at the mountain's peak, I remember walking home from school frightened about the nuclear fallout if a war were ever to break out.

The villa that grew over the apartment we used to occupy now is the one place on the block that does not belong. The paint on the outside is peeling, laundry is hanging on a gauche clothesline out front, and there is graffiti on the wall that runs in front of the property. Grand homes that have risen on either side underscore the deterioration even more. The new villas stand on what used to be empty wooded lots, where couples used to come to make out, and where I dodged turtles and once picked mushrooms with my grandfather. Down the hill, past more expensive houses with high walls and well-kept gardens, I find the old church, whose high gates we once used as goalposts. The church seems to have come back to life, and I imagine that its priest would chase us away were we to set up a game of soccer here now. An old friend's modest home is here too, but looks dark and abandoned.

A game of soccer is being organized at the field of the local soccer team. I am as excited to play as I am anxious about not having the proper shoes. The soles of the one pair of sneakers I own flap back to expose half my foot. Only the thought of a long row of Nikes in the storage room belonging to the owners of our house keeps me from panicking. Sitting in that back room, I try on one pair after another, each time convincing myself that the next pair will not be too big. When I finally make it to the game, I am in shorts and my leather ankle boots.

To match the expensive development, or perhaps because local elections are coming up, the municipality of Nea Penteli is renovating the town square. The town has already built a sidewalk and added streetlights to a stretch of road that had neither and which I once took to school each morning. There is burgeoning construction in the low hills around the square, but down below things look the same, with a few modest shops and even fewer people. In the nearby schoolyard, the boys are playing basketball, not soccer, and the girls, as always, stand apart, now practicing a folk dance. The flag of the European Union, twelve yellow stars arranged in a circle on a blue background, flies alongside the Greek one. The wall around the school is covered with the familiar political graffiti, but now there are also a lot of apolitical, nonsensical, American-style tags. Among the scrawlings, there is also the name of the neofascist, anti-immigrant fringe group, Golden Dawn, and a swastika.

In the twenty years since I last lived here, the city's building sprawl has reached Mount Pentelikon, nullifying much of what separated Nea Penteli from the rest of Athens: trees, clean air, and a comfortable distance from urban problems. This suburb

overlooks the rest of the Greek capital from an elevation that
may suggest to its residents that they are still shielded from
the conditions down below. But the graffiti on the school's
outer wall speaks of a transformation in Nea Penteli that has
now progressed too far to stop. The city has not only reached
this neighborhood; it has been here long enough to generate
the kind of hatred toward the outside that finds expression in a
swastika and that energizes groups like Golden Dawn. And
here, as everywhere in Athens, the pressure from the outside
seems to have convinced many young people to abandon the
group politics of right and left for the refuge of some individu-
alized identity encapsulated in an indecipherable tag. Everything still seems familiar in Nea Penteli; but nothing is the
same.

> The taxi, which will take us to the airport, is loaded up. I
> sit between my parents in the backseat. My baby sister is
> on my mother's lap. From the side and then from the rear
> windows, I wave to my aunt and to my two cousins. They
> stand in the road crying.

The dread of the past comes not so much from the memory
itself. In the lemon tree that still grows, the old schoolyard,
and the apartment now rented to someone else, the landscape
of my inner, private world jumps out of me. The memory, re-
called a million times—its edges dulled by remembrance—
which I have taught myself to pick up, but also to put down, is
now difficult to hold. Past and present intersect, and there is a
reckoning. What recollection has rendered dreamy was real. I
was the boy under the tree, in the schoolyard, on the balcony

of that apartment. The memories have meant so much to me, but those old landmarks just stand there now in stony disregard. These sights cannot help me. Nothing can undo what happened. Perhaps I have known this, but I have not wanted to face it, settling instead to live among the memories, enduring their pain. Because remembering has been easier than accepting, than giving in to the life these places helped forge.

ACKNOWLEDGMENTS

In ancient, if not in modern, Athens, neither mortals nor gods were ever beyond the mysterious reach of Moira—destiny. Moira, it seems to me, played her part in getting my manuscript into the hands of Paul Elie, senior editor with North Point Press and Farrar, Straus and Giroux. I am grateful to him for the sensitivity and insight with which he approached my work. I should also like to thank the kindhearted Mildred Marmur for guiding me through the business of publishing.

I might never have written about Athens had I not embarked on my own journey of self-discovery. Along the way, I have been aided by Dr. June Gray and inspired by the writings of Joseph Campbell. I am fortunate to be sharing the fruits of this journey with Suzy Spence, whose love and support I cherish.

My friends sustained me throughout the period of writing and publishing this book. The love and encouragement of Kostas Kouris and Linda Sachs kept me moving through the streets of Athens. Greg Duncan greeted my idea for this book with genuine excitement and made an apt suggestion for its publication. I am also thankful for the friendship of Nikos Andriotis, Duncan Boothby, Charles Giraudet, Heather Kouris, Kris Maher, Joseph McAndrew, Manolis Saridakis, and Constantine Stamidis. In Athens, I was embraced by Elias Papaioannou, Fotis and Ntanti Gasparatos, Efi Hakiami, Vangelis Patras, Iannis Samakidis, and Elena Papanicolaou. Eliza Jackson was kind to take me as her boarder. I should also like to thank the writer Toby Stein, whom I have never met but whose help from afar I shall not forget.